Pray and Time

NORRIS HALL

Pray and Time

Copyright © 2022 by Norris Hall. All rights reserved.

No part of this publication may be reproduced, stored in a retrieval system or transmitted in any way by any means, electronic, mechanical, photocopy, recording or otherwise without the prior permission of the author except as provided by USA copyright law.

The opinions expressed by the author are not necessarily those of URLink Print and Media.

1603 Capitol Ave., Suite 310 Cheyenne, Wyoming USA 82001
1-888-980-6523 | admin@urlinkpublishing.com

URLink Print and Media is committed to excellence in the publishing industry.

Book design copyright © 2022 by URLink Print and Media. All rights reserved.

Published in the United States of America
Library of Congress Control Number: 2022904754
ISBN 978-1-68486-133-0 (Paperback)
ISBN 978-1-68486-134-7 (Digital)
22.02.22

CHAPTER 1

WHAT IS PRAYER

Prayer is a conversation of the heart with God. Through Prayer, we align ourselves with our Creator, and His presence is revealed to us. We grow in our love and worship of Him. In addition, when we are united with our Lord through prayer, our life becomes fuller, Richer, more joyous, and more peaceful.

1. Prayer is a cleaning process, washing our thoughts feelings, motives, and will, purifying the entire being including the heart, thus enabling us to see

2. God, for without purity no one can see God.

Prayer as, "Prayer is the key to the morning, Noon and Evening. There is no peace without the grace of God, and there is no grace of God without prayer." Grace of God without prayer, many people feel profoundly calm after praying. Prayer is deeply relaxing, and those who do it regularly are meditating. However, cannot explain some remarkable studies showing that to a degree that goes way beyond coincidence, prayer works, It's Praying Time.

Prayer is what you do when you are done struggling with a problem, and you are ready to call forth its solution. Prayer is not about trying to get God to do something to you or give something to you. It is about allowing God to do something through you.

Having a spirit prayer is one of the most important things in our walk with Christ. We must be meditative and contemplatives, listening to Him speak. When we do this, our life is changed. When we pray in the spirit, we are in prayer in our whole life, not just our "prayer" time. We are praying as we work, as we play, as we spend time alone and as we spend time with friends and family.

"A good prayer life, in my estimation, is being aware of God's presence. "Sometimes involves a formal audible prayer, but more often it is a thought life that is shared with God."

We Christians learn to pray through Jesus Christ, who not only teaches us to pray, but prayed himself. Examples of His prayer fill, the Gospels. Did Jesus himself have to learn to pray? Yes, he did. True, he was the Son of God who knew all things. Notice the order in this prayer. First Jesus praises God then he makes his requests. Praising God first puts us in the right frame of mind to tell him about our needs. Too often our prayers are more like shopping lists than conversations. These verses focus on three aspects of prayer: its content, our persistence, and God faithfulness.

God's provision is daily, not once and for all. We cannot store it up and then cut off communication with God, and we dare not be self-satisfied. If you are running low on strength, ask your self-how long have I been away from the Source? When Jesus taught his disciples to pray, he made forgiveness the cornerstone of their relationship with God. God has forgiven our sins; we must now forgive those who have wronged us. To remain unforgiving shows, we have not understood that we ourselves deeply to be forgiven. Think of some people who have wronged you. Have you truly forgiven them? How will God deal with you if he treats you as you treat others?

(Luke 11:1-4) Jesus teaches his disciples about prayer: And it came to pass, that, as he was praying in a certain place, when he ceased, one of his disciples said unto him, Lord, teach us to pray, as John also taught his disciples. And he said unto them, when ye pray, say, Our Father which art in Heaven, Hallowed be thy name. Thy kingdom come, thy will be done, as in heaven, so in earth. Give us day by day our daily bread. And forgive us our sins; for we also forgive every one that is indebted to us. And lead us not into temptation but deliver us from evil.

Yet even in his earliest years. Jesus prayed to God with a distinct intimacy. God was his Father, and he was God's son. There was childlike, filial to his prayer. Jesus prayed regularly his first disciples recalled. He prayed before decisive moments, beginning with his baptism and as he faced his passion and death. He prayed in times of human weakness and death, as he did at the grave of Lazarus. He frequently prayed to give thanks. His prayer was steady, thankful, and confident that God's will was for his good. (Matthew 26:34-41) Jesus said unto him, Verily I say unto thee, that this night, before the cock crow, thou shalt deny me thrice. Peter said unto him, though I should die with thee.

Yet will I not deny thee. Like also all the disciples. Then cometh Jesus with them unto a place called Gethsemane, and saith unto the disciples, sit here, while I go and pray yonder. And he took with him Peter and the two sons of Zebedee and began to be sorrowful and very heavy. Then saith he unto them, my soul is exceeding sorrowful, even unto death: terry ye here, and watch with me. And he went a little farther, and fell on his face, and prayed, saying, O my father, if it be possible, let this cup pass from me; nevertheless not as I will, but as thou wilt. And he cometh unto the disciples, and find them asleep, and saith unto Peter, what, could ye not watch with me one hour? Watch and pray that ye enter not into temptation: the spirit indeed is willing, but the flesh is weak.

His prayer was heartfelt. Nowhere is that more evident than when he prayed on the cross. "Father, forgive them, for they know not what they do." I thirst." Jesus was not rebelling against his Father's will when he asked that the cup of suffering and separation be taken away. In fact, he reaffirmed his desire to do God's will by saying, "Nevertheless not as I will, but as thou wilt." His prayer reveals to us his terrible suffering. His agony was worse than death as he paid for all sin by being separated from God. The sinless Son of God took our sins upon himself to save us from suffering and separation.

In times of suffering people sometimes wish they knew the future, or they wish they could understand the reason for their anguish. Jesus knew what lay ahead of him, and he knew the reason. Even so, his struggle was intense-more wrenching than any struggle we will ever have to face. What does it take to be able to say "Thy will be done"? It takes trust in God pains, prayer, and obedience each step of the way.

Jesus used Peter's drowsiness to warn him about the kinds of temptation he would soon face. The way to overcome temptation is to be alert to it and pray. Alert means being aware of the possibilities of temptation sensitive to the subtleties. Prayer can release our tensions in times of emotional stress, many people don't pray because they think that they can fix the problem. As long as you think you can fix it God will not here you. Pray changes things if you know pray changes things you must have faith that prayer will change things there are something that will hinder prayer first check out the person in the morrow.

(a) Selfishness will hinder prayer

(b) Unbelief will hinder prayer

(c) Unforgiving spirit will hinder prayer many people go without answers to prayers because they have wronged others.

There are people try to cover up their sins, don't want nobody to know what they are doing. But God see you He is knocking on the door of your heart, he wants to have fellowship with you, open up to him. He is patient and persistent trying to get through to you, he does not do breaking and entering, but he is knocking. He allows us a decide whether or not to open our life to him.

We often wish we could escape troubles, the pain of grief, the loss, the sorrow and failure, even the small daily frustrations that constantly wear us down. It praying time, we learn that the world is a tremendous battleground where the forces under Satan's power and those under God's authority are at war. Satan and his forces are motivated by bitter hated for Christ and his forces. Jesus prayed for his disciples, including those of us who follow him today. Jesus prayed that God would keep his chosen believers safe from Satan's power, making them pure and holy, uniting them through his truth. (Revelation 3:20) Jesus said Behold, I stand at the door, and knock: if any man hear my voice, and open the door, I will come in to him, and will sup with him, and he with me, It's Praying Time. The Laodiceans church was complacent and rich. They felt self-satisfied, but they didn't have Christ's presence among them. He knocked at the door of their hearts, but they were busy enjoying world pleasures that they didn't notice that Jesus was trying to enter. The pleasures of this world-money, security, material possessions-can be dangerous, because their temporary satisfaction makes us indifferent to God's offer of lasting satisfaction.

If you find yourself feeling indifferent to church, to God, or to the Bible, you have begun to shut God out of your life. Leave the door of your heart constantly open to God and you won't need to worry about missing his knock. Let him in is your only hope for lasting fulfillment. Jesus prayed for all who would follow him.

His prayer was heartfelt, nowhere is that more evident than when he prayed on the cross. "Father, forgive them, for they know not what they do. I thirst, Woman, behold your son. Son, behold your mother." My God, my God why have you forsaken me?" "It is finished." "Father, into your hands I commend my spirit."

They were prayers that came from the heart. They reveal him tender towards those he loved and forgiving to those who wronged him; he is human in weakness and strong in faith. Never did a human heart reach out to God more eloquently than when Jesus prayed on the cross. He ended his life with a loud cry. Even that last rending cry was a heartfelt prayer to God, issuing from the depths of his being and summing up what could not say. In addition, his prayer was heard. God raised him up. We Christians believe the prayer of Jesus teaches that prayer is always heard. In his prayer is our hope.

What can we learn from the prayers of Jesus? First, that **true Prayer should come from the heart.** He prayed from within, not with just words or gestures. His prayer was not based only on feelings or passing emotions. Prayer comes from within, beyond level of feelings, from us. "Go into the inner room, "Jesus says, "and there pray to your Father, who hears you."

Sometimes pray from the heart, from the "inner room" takes the form of words, at other times it may be like his wordless cry. Secondly, **Prayer is fed by Faith.** Jesus prayed with an unwavering faith in his heavenly Faith, a faith that lasted until his death. He taught us to pray also with childlike faith in God, believing that the one who loves us hears our prayers.

Thirdly, **Prayer should be steady and persevering** as his prayer was even when no answer comes or when no relief is in sight. **"Watch and pray," he says Seek and knock. It's Praying Time" the door that reveals God's Holy will be opened.**

The disciples asked Jesus to teach them to pray, he did, and he teaches us too. He answered by teaching them the prayers we call the Lord's Prayer. The Lord's Prayer is a basic Christian pray, as a model of prayer, every Christian leans it by heart. It appears everywhere in the church's life: in its liturgy and sacraments. public and private. It is a prayer all Christians treasure.

Paul and the new Christians at Thessalonica experienced persecution because of their faith in Christ. Christians expect trials and troubles as well. The Holy Spirit helps us to remain strong in faith, we are able to show genuine love to others and it help you and I to maintain our moral character even when we are being persecuted, slandered or oppressed.

We need to stand firm in faith in the midst of trials during let the Holy Spirit Strengthened you.

Paul expressed his concern for the church even while he was being slandered. All believers both those who are alive and those who have died will be united with Christ. No one knows the time of Christ return we are to live Holy lives, Stand Firm, Work and live to please the Lord. Don't let him caught you with your work undone.

It's Praying Time. Evening and morning and at noon will I pray and cry aloud and he shall hear my voice. God is moving all over this world. Saying turn from your sinful ways this is what corid-19 is all about, turn to God while you have a chance.

Our sins bring pressures up on us our own sins cause many of our troubles. Prayer is our best help when trials come our way because it keeps us in communion with some people worry too much, give it to God. He is able to carry all of our worries our stress, our struggles, just take it to the Lord in prayer.

Though we memorize it as a set formula, the Lord's Prayer should not be repeated mechanically or without though. Its purpose is to awaken and stimulate our faith. Through this prayer, Jesus invites us to approach God as Father. Indeed, the Lord's Prayer has been called a summary of the gospel. When Moses approached God on Mount Sinai, he heard a voice saying. "Do not come near; pull off your shoes from your feet, for the place on which you are standing is holy ground." An infinite chasm separates us from the transcendent God.

In the Lord's Prayer, Jesus invites us to draw near to God who is beyond understanding, who dwells in mystery, who is all-holy. We can call God". Calling God "Father" does not mean that God is masculine. God is beyond the categories of gender, of masculine or feminine. None of our descriptions of God is adequate. God, who is "in heaven", whose name is holy, cannot be fully known by us.

By calling God "Father," we are more rightly describing ourselves and our relationship with God. Jesus teaches that we have a filial relationship with God; God sees us as if we were a daughter or a son. In addition, we on our part can approach God in the familiar confident way a child approaches a loving parent. What is more, we approach God through God's only Son, Jesus Christ, who unites us to himself.

Thy Kingdom come, thy will be done, on earth as it is in heaven, God's kingdom. Jesus often said that God's power would appear and renew all creation. God like a mighty king would rule over the earth according to a plan that unfolds from the beginning of the world. Peace and justice would mark God's kingdom. Good would be rewarded and evil punished. The kingdom, according to Jesus, is not far off, but already present in our midst, though not yet revealed. It is a daily battle. Trials like sickness and failure can crush out spirits. False values and easy promises can entice us and even destroy our souls. Therefore, we ask God to keep us from failing when we are tested, to help know the right thing to do, to deliver us from evil, which awaits us in life.

The Lord's Prayer sums up the teaching of Jesus. It is also a prayer that offers the grace of Jesus: his reverence for God, his child like confidence in his Father, and his power to go bravely through life no matter what comes. When we pray his prayer, his spirit becomes our own.

Yet Jesus is more than a teacher. As Christians we believe that Jesus prays for us: he is our intercessor before God. As Savior, he gathers our prayers, our needs, and the cries of our hearts to make them his own and offers them to God who hears our prayers, in the prayer of his daughter and sons. That is why we complete our prayer so often with the beautiful phrases: "Through Jesus Christ, our Lord. Amen." Jesus is our teacher and he is our Savior, who takes our prayers and makes them his own, after your prayers, start your work let your deeds and everywhere, sees all your actions, doings feeling, thoughts and desires, and will generously reward for all your good. "Prayer is the answer to every problem in life. It puts us in tune with divine wisdom which knows how to adjust everything perfectly. So often, we do not pray in certain situation, because from our standpoint the outlook is hopeless. However, nothing is impossible with God. Nothing is so entangled that it cannot be remedied.

No human relationship is too strained for God to bring about human reconciliation and understanding, no habit so deep rooted that it cannot be overcome: No one is so weak that he or she cannot be strong, no one is so ill that he or she cannot be healed. No mind is so dull that it cannot be made brilliant. Whatever we need if we trust God, He will supply it. If anything is causing worry or anxiety, let us stop rehearsing the difficulty and trust God for healing, love and power. Psalm 108:13) Through God we shall do valiantly: for he it is that shall tread down our enemies.

Prayers end wither quests for help to make it through stressful situations? David prayed not merely for rescue. But for victory, with God's help we can claim more than just survival, we can claim victory! Look for ways God can use your distress as an opportunity to show his mighty power. Though Satan's power may temporarily increase, we are not too led astray. God is all—powerful, He is in control. He will bring his true family safely into eternal life. Because he cares for us, we can trust him with our very life, assurance of Christ's return gives suffering Christians the strength to endure. We can look forward to his return as King and Judge. Since no one knows the time when he will appear, we must be ready at all times by keeping our faith strong.

God is omnipresent he is present everywhere. Because this is so, you can never be lost to his Spirit. This is good news to those who know and love God, because no matter what we do or where we go, we can never be far from God's comforting presence. (Psalm 5:1-2) Give ear to my words O LORD, consider my meditation. (2) Hearken unto the voice of my cry, my King, and my God: for unto thee will I pray. God answered Hezekiah's prayer and delivered Judah by sending an angel to attack the Assyrian camp, forcing Sennacherib to leave at once. Prayer should be our first response in any crisis. Don't wait until things are hopeless. Pray daily for his guidance. Our problem are God's opportunities, (Ezra Ch 8:23) and I said unto them, Ye are holy unto the LORD; the vessels are holy also; and the silver and the gold are a freewill offering unto the LORD God of your fathers.

I have learned so many times just before God bless, He will stand back and let storms come in our life. We have got to trust Jesus and keep the Faith. Storm don't last all ways. Song say trouble don't last all ways we're going to have some struggles in this life. The good days our weigh our bad days. I know Jesus as a supplier, I know he can heal the sick and raise the dead. But they had never met Jesus in a storm, they did not recognize Him. He will show up and wipe your tears away. He will show up to let you know that you are not along. He wants us to have faith and believe in him. Take courage in spite of struggles run on the victory has already been won. Where was their trust in God? We have got to learn to focus on God's faithfulness in the past, so we can face crises with confidence rather than with fear.

You will never walk along when you place your faith in Jesus. He places his spirit before, behind and within you. God never sends you out alone. He never experienced being away from his father the two had been one for eternity. He prayed He faced his ultimate fear with hones prayers. I wonder how many burdens Jesus are carrying for us that we know nothing about. He carries our sins, He carries our shame, he carries our eternal debt. And how often do we thank him for his kindness. The world events may seem out of control and Justice may seem scarce, but God is in control.

God is able, He know our sitting down, our standing up, He know our thoughts, He knows what in our heart, He know what on our minds, If I go to heaven God is there. If I make my bed in Hell He is there be encourage no matter what we are going through. God is able to carry you through. Out of all David went through He kept a humble attitude when you dwell on your problems you will become anxious, and angry. David said I will bless the Lord at all times. Unlike David, God wants to carry our burdens but so often we continue to carry them ourselves, even when we say that we trust him we mass up so many times.

David knew real help comes from God alone when a situation seen out of control God will never forsake those who trust in him. How do you know? Because God's promise never to leave us, He wants us when we are going to the storms of life. He will never leave us no matter what we face. We are just like David tries to save our own selves David learned that he had to turn around and lean on God. I can tell you all day long how good God is, but you want no until you tried him for yourself. Let us look at this passage of scripture today I believe that the one thing that holds our attention in this amazing story are the impossible of how Jesus took two little fish and loaves of bread, and blessed it, brake the loaves and gave them to his disciples to set before them, sat them down in groups of 100 and by 50's. And the two fish were divided among them all. They did all eat and were filled. We are dealing with the impossibilities with two fish five loaves. He fled 5,000 men not counting women and children and then had left over.

When Jesus asked the disciples to provide food for all these people said it would take a fortune to feed all these people. We are dealing with the impossibilities with two fish, five loaves, when Jesus asked the disciples to provide food for all these people. They said it would take a fortune to feed all these people. This was a situation that was impossible for man. But it was an opportunity for Jesus. The disciples had some experience with Jesus already, but never feeding an army of people with two fish-five loaves. Are the impossibilities of how Jesus took two little fish and loaves of bread, and blessed brake the loaves and gave them to his disciples to set before them sat them down in groups, and the two fishes divided he among them all they did all ate and were filled. We are dealing with the impossibilities with two fish, five loaves when Jesus asked the disciples to provide food for all these people. They said it would take a fortune to feed all these people.

This was a situation that was impossible for man, but it was an opportunity for God. The disciples had some experience with Jesus already, but never feeding an army of people with two fish, five loaves. Why did Jesus bother to feed these people he could have easily sent them on their way, Jesus does not ignore needs, like some people, he listing to all our needs. (Philippians 4:19) But my God shall supply all your need according to his riches in glory by Christ Jesus. We can trust that God will always meet our needs. Whatever we need on earth he will always supply, there is a difference between our wants and our needs. We may not get all that we want, by trusting in Christ, our attitudes and appetites can change from wanting everything to accepting his provision and power to live for him.

CHAPTER

GOD STILL ANSWER PRAYERS

Wisdom is only effective when it is put into action early in Solomon life he recognizes his need for wisdom. By the time Solomon asked for wisdom to rule his kingdom he had already started a habit which would make his wisdom ineffective for his own life. He sealed a pact with Egypt by marrying Pharaoh's daughter he went against not only his father's last words. But God's direct commands his action reminds us how easy it is to know what is right and still doing wrong. It is clear that God's gift of wisdom to Solomon did not mean that he couldn't make mistakes, David ask to build a Temple first God said no. God wanted a peace maker not a warrior to build his house of prayer.

(1 King Ch3:5-6) Solomon was given a chance to have anything in the world and he asked for wisdom and understanding heart. In order to make right decisions we can ask God for this same wisdom that should be in our prayer. Lord blessed me with wisdom, knowledge, and understanding. Solomon prayed for wisdom and God made him wiser than anyone else had ever been.

We need wisdom but even more we need a steadfast relationship with God, He is the source of all wisdom. Not everyone has great wisdom, but all have the opportunity to be faithful to God, (2 Chronicles Ch 6:18-19) But will God in very deed dwell with men on the earth?

Behold, heaven and the heaven of heavens cannot contain thee; how much less this house which I have built.

(Vs. 19) have respect therefore to the prayer of thy servant, and to his supplication, O Lord my God, to hearken unto the cry and the prayer which thy servant prayed before thee.

The Temple was a place where the people could worship God. God did not need a Temple to live in, because not even the highest heaven could contain Him. At the Temple God was present in a special way among his people, we can praise God and pray anywhere at any time. God was reaching out to us in love through his Son Jesus Christ, God want us to reach out to him in love. Only then will we come to love him with all our hearts, take time to get to know him.

We are just like Solomon when we realize we have sinned, when we realize we have sinned that should drive us to God forgiveness. (Psalm 14:3) They are all gone aside they are all together become filthy there is none that doeth good no not one. We are Save by the Grace of God no one but God is perfect, all of us stand guilty before God and need his forgiveness.

No matter how well we perform none of us can boast about our goodness it's not you or I, it is God get the glory. Jesus is the only perfectly man, since we fall short we must turn to Christ to save us. Solomon's dedication of the Temple is a Picture of the way each of us should dedicate ourselves to the special purpose God has given to us. God purpose is to offer salvation to the world, God is in charge not you or I.

Months maybe years had passed since Solomon's prayer of dedication. After all this time God told Solomon that I had heard his prayer. After all this time God told Solomon that he had heard his prayer, but nothing happens I wonder if God heard me. God does hear and he will provide for us he will answer your prays at the proper time. God still answer prayers when Solomon prayed, ask God to make provisions for the people when they sinned. God answered with four conditions for forgiveness,

(1) I want you to humble yourself by admitting your sins.

(2) Pray to God asking for forgiveness.

(3) Seek God continually.

(4) Turn from your sinful behavior God will answer our prayers

God is moving all over this world saying turn to me. God appeared to Solomon by night told him, I have heard thy prayer. After the temple was completed Solomon prayed a pray of dedication, His pray was concerning a variety of situations Solomon asked God to make provisions for the people when they sinned. God did make that provisions when he sent his son Jesus Christ. I believe years had pass since Solomon prayed a prayer of provision.

God told Solomon I heard thy prayer I had not forgot you, If my people which are called by my name shall humble themselves, pray and seek my face, and turn from their wicked ways then will I hear from heaven, and I will forgive their sins, and will heal their land. God still answer prays, It's Praying Time.

After the temple dedication, fire came down from heaven and consumed the burnt offering and the sacrifices. Fire will not come down anymore, if we repent and pray the holy spirt will come down, so we pray to God Almighty as our Redeemer and Savior, seeking His will in our lives and having faith that He will provide for our every need. (Psalm 37:4) assures us of this: "Delight thyself also in the Lord; and he shall give thee the desires of thine heart."

If our prayers were answered for the wrong reasons, we would continue to pray to God for what we get from Him. We would continue to pray so we could gain material goods. Our selfishness would be fed we would not recognize that we should surrender our lives to God. When we ask of God, we should in His name for His will to be done. Jesus tells us in (John 16:23-24), "I tell you the truth my Father will give you whatever you ask in his name. Until now, you have not asked for anything in my name. Ask and you will receive, and your joy will be complete." When we do that, we hand Him our selfishness, our desire for control, our desire for worldly possessions. We have a feeling of love that is a result of God redeeming us from our sins.

(Ezra Ch 8:23) So we fasted and besought our God for this: and he was interested in us. Ezra knew God's promises to protect his people, but he didn't take them for granted. He also knew that God's blessings were appropriated through prayer. And their prayers were answered. Fasting humbled them because going without food reminded them of their complete dependence on God's provision. Fasting also gave complete dependence on God's provision. You cannot be saved without faith (John3:36). You cannot live victoriously over the world without faith, (1 John 5:4). You cannot please God without faith (Hebrews 11:6). You cannot pray without faith you cannot have peace with God without faith (Romans 5:1). You cannot have joy without faith. (1 Pet 1:8). You are justified by faith and not by works you are to live by faith (Galatians 2). Christ dwells in your heart by faith. The Holy Spirit is received by faith. "Whatever is not from faith is sin Faith is important because it honors God, and God always honors faith. Faith defies reason; it moves mountains (Matt. 17:14-21). face facts; it never gives up. Faith says, "God is working out His perfect will in my life, and I can wait, endure, and suffer." Faith does not make anything easy it does make all things possible. You are covered head to foot with the powerful armor of God. The armor of God is strong stand against any attack of the enemy. Let me show you how it works. And having done all, to stand, stand therefore, having your lions girt about truth." When Satan tells you that you will never see the manifestation of your prayers is the time to gird yourself with the truth. Jesus said Thy God's word is truth (John 17:17) Satan is the liar and father of lies. Determine in your heart that having done all to stand.

God's Word you will not be moved by what you see, hear or think the Word of God only moves you. God is slow to get angry, but when he is ready to punish, even the earth trembles. Often people avoid God because they see evildoers in the world and hypocrites in the church. They do that because God is slow to anger, he gives his true follower time to share his love evildoers. God is letting us know, that He will be with us in our trouble I will be with you when storms comes in your lives. When we give up get out of the way, we cannot weather our storms.

You have stayed awake at night, worrying about the storm in your life God will show up in your storm, he is encouraging those who suffer for Him to trust him. Because we never know what kind of storm, we will meet in this life. And I know that God gives the grace to enable us to rejoice in a storm. We are rejoicing only because we know that God somehow, some way, will see us through. Prayer is an attitude it involves more than just making requests. Prayer is communicating with God. You can live in an attitude of prayer constantly, being in communion and fellowship with your heavenly Father every hour of the day.

In order to get results in prayer, you must be convinced of one basic fact: God wants to answer your prayers. In fact, He is as ready and willing to answer you, as He was to answer Jesus during His early ministry. This may be difficult for you to believe, but it is true. I remember how amazed I was to learn about God's willingness to answer my prayers. I had always thought of myself as unworthy. I thought, why would God bother to answer my prayers? Ignorance of God's Word kept me from receiving His best in my life. Once I realized the importance of the Word of God, my attitude changed. I realized that God does not see His children as unworthy. Notice how Jesus prayed…that the world may know that thou hast sent me, and hast loved them, as thou hast loved me" (John 17:23).

Just think! God loves you as much as he loves Jesus! **We are worthy!** Knowing that God is ready to answer your prayers will make you serious about your prayer life. Never take your prayer privilege lightly. Because you are a child of God, you have an open invitation from Him to come into the throne room any time you wish. We do not have to enter His presence crawling on your hands and knees. We can boldly stand before God without a sense of guilt or shame or condemnation.

Let us therefore come boldly unto the throne of grace that we may obtain mercy, and find grace to help in time of need. (Hebrews 4:16) When we understand what pray is, it helps you to realize what it is, it is not an emotional release. It is not an escape ring. It is much more than asking God to do something for you or have God do me a favor. Prayer is not a religious favor from God, when we pray it should be for results.

Jesus said in (Matthew 6:7) when ye pray, use not vain repetitions, as the heathen do: for they think that they shall be heard for their much speaking." The big long words do not get the ear of God. He responds to faith. To explain, let me give you an example from my own experience. Not long after I become a Christian, I asked a Preacher to pray for me. I was expecting to here a long beautiful prayer one that would cause people to fall on their knees in repentance before God! He laid his hand on my head, bowed his head. And said, "Lord bless her. Meet her every need Amen." He then turned and walked away. I was left standing there thinking how could he do that to me? I had a big problem one major difference separated that minister and me: the degree of faith at work in our live. He was operating in faith, praying exactly what he meant. I was a baby Christian, looking for a physical to help me. It makes no difference how long you pray or how beautiful your words. When we have faith that mean we are having confidence in God, and his power to answer our prayers. (Hebrews 11:1) "Now faith is the substance of things hoped for, the evidence of things not seen." Hope is always in the future faith is always now. We often wish we could escape troubles of this world, the pain, the loss, the sorrow, and the failure. If God didn't give us no rough roads to walk, if he didn't give us no mountains to climb.

If he didn't give us no battles to fight, we wouldn't grow. Some time it takes trials and tribulation to keep us humble. Some time it takes trials to keep us on our knees. Down through this, somebody had some bad days, and Somebody had some good days. But thank God we are still here. God promises to carry us through He promise to be with us. He promises never to leave us. No cross, no crown, everybody want a crown. But nobody wants to bear there cross.

Jesus used this picture of his followers taking up their crosses to follow him. Following Jesus mean a true commitment, no turning back take up our cross and follow Jesus means to be willing to publicly identify with him. Be willing to face even suffering for his sake Jesus said and he that taketh not his cross and follower after me. Is not worthy of me, how God can be measured by how well we treat one other. Jesus tells us if we cannot not bear our cross and come after Him we cannot be his disciple.

We do not deserve any of God blessing but he loves us so much until he still shows us favor. Even in the middle of our storm God is right there two show us favor (Psalm 30:5) for his anger "endureth" but a moment in his favor is life. The discomfort of God's anger is momentary let God's anger be a brief discomfort don't let God keep being anger with you God does not play. Don't take God for grant, what separates us from God is sin, no matter how good we think we are every person is guilty of sin, God doesn't want us to be separated from him so He made a way to fix what's broken. That is the only way through faith, in Jesus Christ, according to the scriptures anyone can be saved, forgiven by God and guaranteed heaven through FAITH in Jesus Christ. The only way a person can find salvation is by accepting Jesus Christ as their Savior.

Why was he troubled? He knew all his riches and his power had come from God. All his riches had gone to his head making him proud, his wealth, his power, he was secure and independent of God He didn't need God anymore, it was like I have everything I don't need God. The grace of God is the favor of God and the grace of God cause good things to happen in our lives through the channel of faith. Even those who did not believe in him recognized that he enjoyed the favor of God.

God seeks out those who love Him and love his commands so that he can bless, guide, and protect them. This does not mean that everyone who is prosperous or healthy has found favor with God. A good person is one who follows God, and one who trust him. God watches over and directs every step that we take because he fine favor in you.

Many people in the Bible had the Lord Favor, but also suffered hardship, God is not working to make us happy but to fulfill his purpose. The Lord invites us to seek his favor and when we seek his favor, we humble our hearts before him see him for himself not just for the blessings He give. God want you to love him with all our heart, soul, mind and strength (Proverbs 8:35) For those who find me find life and receive favor from the Lord.

For His anger endureth but a moment in his favor is life weeping may endure for a night, but joy cometh in the morning. He did not say He would come at every call. Keep the Faith be patient your morning is coming, just trust him, hold on and keep the faith.

Some believers falsely assume that lots of material possessions are a sign of God's spiritual blessing. The Laodicea was a wealthy city the church was also wealthy. But what the Laodiceans could see and buy had become more valuable to them than what is unseen and eternal. Money can make people feel confident satisfied but no matter how much you possess or how much money you make, you have nothing if you don't have a relationship with Jesus Christ. Amen

I counsel thee to buy of me gold tried in the fire that thou mayest be rich, and white raiment that thou may be clothed and that the shame of thy nakedness do not appear, and anoint thine eyes with eye salve that thou may see.

Jesus is talking about the Laodicea was known for its great wealth. Jesus was telling them to buy their gold from him. (Real spiritual treasures), He told them to purchase white garment from him also these people had an eye problem. But Jesus told them to get medicine from him to heal their eyes so they could see the truth (Revelation Ch 3: 19) I rebuke and punish all whom I love. God would discipline this lukewarm church unless they turned from their indifference toward him. His purpose in discipline is not to punish, but to bring people back to him. Are you lukewarm in your devotion to God? God may discipline you to help you out of your uncaring attitude, but he uses only loving discipline. You can avoid God's discipline by drawing near to him again through confession, service, worship, and studying his word just as the spark of love can be rekindled in marriage so the Holy Spirit can reignite our zeal for God when we allow him to work in our heart.

So many are like the Laodicea church, they are so busy enjoying worldly pleasures that they are not notice that Jesus is trying to enter. The pleasures of this world-money, security, material possessions- can be dangerous, because their temporary satisfaction makes us indifferent to God's offer of lasting satisfaction. If you find yourself feeling indifferent to church, to God, or to the Bible, you have begun to shut God out of your life. Leave the door of your heart constantly open to God and you won't need to worry about missing his knock. Letting him in is your only hope for lasting fulfillment.

Jesus is knocking on the door of our heart every time we sense we should turn to him. He wants to have fellowship with us, and he wants us to open up to him. He is patient and persistent in trying to get through to us-not breaking and entering, but knocking. He allows us to decide whether or not to open our life to him.

The gospel shows us both how righteous God is in his plan for us to be saved, and also how we may be made fit for eternal life. By trusting Christ our relationship with God is made right from faith to faith means that from start to finish God declares us to be righteous because of faith, and faith alone. God's glory is the revelation of his character and presence. The lives of Jesus disciples reveal his character and he is present to the world through them. Paul was not boasting when he gave God the credit for all his accomplishment. The false teachers boasted of their own power and success, no one nobody can clams to be adequate without God help

No one can carry out the responsibilities of God's calling in his or her own strength. Without the Holy Spirit we can do nothing for God. We must have his spirit. We often run to God when we experience difficulties, stay in his presence everyday so when troubles come your way you are in his presence. You are prepared to handle any test many of our problems could be avoided or handled easily by seeking God's help beforehand. Stop saying I got it, I can do it, we can't do anything on our own. That is why so many have not got there blessing, because I can do it. Move out of the way, God does not need our help. No matter how much they have it will fade and vanish like grass that withers and dies our treasures will be in heaven what we get from following God lasts forever. Even thou sometimes our burdens seem more we can go on.

This was a promise to God's earthly people He told them don't worry about the wicked you trust in me. And I will take care of you the weight thyself also in the Lord and he shall give thee the desires of thine heart. This was a promise for Israel and it also applies to us today, God has already blessed us with spiritual blessings, and He will shower on you and I all the spiritual blessings you can contain, Then notice what we are to do we are to delight ourselves in the Lord. (Vs.

5) commit thy way unto the Lord trust also, commit thy way unto the Lord, many Christians criticize and find fault with God. Why because they have not committed their ways to the Lord.

Trust also in him and he shall bring it to pass. Give God time He knows your problems, He sees every tear that fall from your eyes. Commit yourself, wait he do not move because of our problems or because we are crying. He moves because he loves us and that love works on his time not our time. Wait commit yourself he will work things out in your life, He is our Father, He is our Friend, He love us, He wants to save us, but we have to commit our ways to him rest in the Lord. How do I rest in the Lord and wait patient for him (Ezra 8:21) Then I proclaimed a fast there, at the river of Ahava. That we might afflict ourselves before our God to seek of him a right way for us and for our little ones, and for all our substance. Ezra and the people traveled approximately 900 miles on foot. The trip took them through dangerous and difficult territory and lasted about four months. They prayed that God would protect them and give them a good journey. Our journeys today may not be as difficult and dangerous as Ezras, but we should recognize our need to ask God for guidance and protection.

Their prayers and fasting, prepared them spiritually by showing their dependence on God for protection, their faith that God was in control, and their affirmation that they were not strong enough to make the trip without him. When we take time to put God first in any endeavor, we are preparing well for whatever lies ahead. Prayer is still God's mighty force in solving problems today. Prayer and action go hand in hand. Through prayer, God guides our preparation, teamwork, and diligent efforts to carry out his will. (Romans 3:24) Being justified freely by his grace through the redemption that is in Christ Jesus.

"Justified freely" means to be declares not guilty. When a judge in a court of law declares the defendant not guilty, all the charges are removed from his record. Legally, it is as if the person had never been accused. When God forgives our sins, our record is wiped clean. It is as though we had never sinned. Jesus prayed for his disciples, including those of us who follow him today. He prayed that God would keep his chosen believers safe from Satan's power, making them pure and holey, uniting them through his truth. Someone ask the question how do we get eternal life? By knowing God, the Father himself through Jesus Christ. Eternal life requires entering onto a personal relationship with God in Jesus Christ. When we admit our sin and turn away from it, Christ's love lives in us by the Holy Spirit. Because He is all-seeing, all-knowing, all-holy, all-present, God knows us better than we know our serves, God is with us and his greatest gift is to allow us to know him. God works out his plans for our lives and will bring us through the difficulties we face. He is with us through every situation in every trial. He is protecting us He love us and knows us completely. God is omnipresent He is present everywhere you can never be lost to his spirt.

We are Christians and we live in the light this then is the message which we have heard of him and declare unto you that God is light, and in him is no darkness at all. Light represents what is good pure, true, holy and reliable. Darkness represents sin and evil God is perfectly holey true and that he alone can guide us out of the darkness of sin.

If we want to have a relationship with God, we must put aside our sinful ways of living. If you find yourself doubting God, remember he want put no more on you than you can bear. Remember before you start doubting God make sure that you have all your facts together, God wants only the best for your life. When you're struggling trying to make it don't ever, assume the worst. (Romans 8:35) who shall separate us from the love of Christ shall tribulation or distress or persecution.

Paul explain that it is impossible to be separated from Jesus Christ. He tells us how great his love is so that we will feel totally secure in him. This is where our faith, believe, and our truth, if we do this, we will not be afraid, God loves us. He knows every step we take every right step every by-step he is acquainted with all our ways and he know what company we walk with. He knows each one of us by name, he knows where we live, he knows how many days we have up on this earth, and he is counting down every day he is counting down. We don't have time to do wrong, don't have time for hate, we don't have much time as we had yesterday.

Trusting in God's care in the mid of fear when everything seems dark his truth still shines bright. When God is far you those against you will never succeed. (Psalm 139: vs 23) David hatred of his enemies came from his zeal for God. David regarded his enemies as God's enemies, so his hatred was a desire for God's righteous justice and not for personal vengeance. Is it all right to be angry with people who hate God? Yes, but we must remember that it is God who will deal with them, not us if we truly love God, then we will be deeply hurt if someone hates him. But we seek justice against evil, we must pray that God's enemies will turn to him before he judges them.

If we open up to him, stop trying to do it our self. Trust in the Lord He want fail you, he is on our side when the storms come in your life he is right there. He will never walk away and leave you, we are the one that will walk away and leave him. He knows our problems he even sees every tear that fall from our eyes. All ways remember that the Lord works on his time not our time. David said wait commit yourself he will work things out in your life, he is our father, he is our friend he loves us. We have committed our ways to the Lord. David said weeping may in due for a night, but joy cometh in the morning. How do I rest in the Lord and wait patiently for him? To commit ourselves to the Lord means to trust him, believing that he can care for us. Better that we can ourselves, we should be willing to wait patiently for him to work out what is best for us.

(1 Peter 5:7) Tells us to cast all our cares upon Jesus, cast all our cares upon Jesus for he cares for you. What are you saying Peter I am saying

carrying your worries and daily struggles by yourself show that you have not committed yourself fully to God (Matthew16:24) Jesus tells us if any man will come after me let him deny himself and take up his cross and follow me, Following Christ means to commit to Him Being his disciple it means putting aside selfish.

The Laodicea is the last of these seven letters, and its name means justice of the people. (Revelation Ch 3:14-22)Philadelphia church, this is the church that had turned back to the word of God, and the words mean brotherly love. Sardis church mean wake and repent. Thyatira mean a continual sacrifice. Ephesus means the desirable one. Smyrna was a fragrant spice, but had to be crushed and beaten, tribulation, poverty, suffer, prison. Pergamos means married it was the church which was married to the world. Thyatira mean literally a continual sacrifice, (Rev 3: 14) And unto the angel of the church of the Laodiceans write these things saith the Amen. The faithful and true witness, the beginning of the creation of God.

This is the only place in Scripture where Amen is a proper name, and it is the name of Christ Jesus. What about all those Scriptures we read and it end with Amen, when the word is preached and you know it is right you say Amen, you are witnessing to the word. When you say Amen to the word, you are saying may it be so, or so it is. But here Jesus calls himself Amen (Isaiah 65:16). He is the God of the Amen (Isaiah 7:9) the word believe is Amen (2 Corinthians 1:20). We read for all the promises of God in him are yea, and in him Amen.

The Lord Jesus is the Amen, He has the last word He is the Alpha and the Omega. He is the one who is going to fulfill all the promises of God, and here he is letting to Laodiceans know this because this is the church that has rejected the deity of Christ (Rev.3: 15). I know thy words that thou are neither cold nor hot. How I wish you were either one of their other. (Rev.3: 16) But because you are lukewarm, neither hot not cold I am going to spit you out of my mouth. Laodicea was the wealthiest of the seven cities known for its banking industry.

Manufacture of wool, and medical school they always had problems with its water supply. God said I will reject you are not hot or cold.

I am going to spit you out of my mouth, stop playing with me stop, being lukewarm, you are hot or you are cold. The church of Philadelphia will be raptured before the tribulation and the church of Thyatira will be cast into tribulation. The church of Laodicea will be utterly rejected of the Lord. But in Laodicea there are some that is save and they will become part of the Philadelphia church. (Rev. 3:17) Because thou sayest I am rich and increased with goods and have need of nothing and know not that thou art wretched, and miserable and poor and blind, and naked. Some believes falsely assume that lots of material possessions are a sign of God spiritual.

(Revelation Ch 4:1) After this I look and behold a door was opened in heaven and the first voice which I heard was as it were of a trumpet talking with me which said come up hither and I will shew thee things which must be hereafter. Jesus knocked at the door of our hearts People are so busy enjoying worldly pleasure that they are not notice that Jesus are trying to enter.

The pleasures of this world can be dangerous, leave the door of your heart open to God, and you won't need to worry about missing his knock. Letting Jesus in is your only hope for everlasting life Jesus is knocking on the door of our heart, he wants to have fellowship with us he wants us to open up to him. He is patient trying to get through to us, he is not going to break and enter but he is knocking. There is power all power on the other size of that door, He said I am knocking on your door please let me in.

John said the first voice that sounded like a trumpet blast was Jesus Christ. In (Rev. 1:10) John said the first voice that sounded like a trumpet blast was Jesus Christ,

John said I was in the spirit on the Lord's and heard behind me a great voice as of a trumpet. Jesus said I'm standing at the door knocking, Jesus said I am knocking on every sinners heart, If you don't know me opening up let me in time is getting short.

Stop saying I'M not ready I want to party some more, support God come while you are parting those people are Hell bound. (2Thessalonians 2ch:3) let no man deceive you by any means for that day shall not come except there Come a falling away first from the church. God want somebody to praise him, the pews can't do it. (2 Peter 3:10) the day of the Lord will come as a thief in the night in which the heavens shall pass away with a great noise and the elements shall melt with fervent heat. The earth also and the works that are there shall be burned up.

The day of the Lord refers to the events that began with Christ's return to catch up the faithful of his churches to meet Him in the air, open up your door of your heart and tell him to come on in. The disciples wanted to know from Jesus when would the end come. Jesus told them to take heed that no man deceive you, many will come in my name saying I am Christ, and shall deceive many. And you shall hear of wars nations against nation, Famines, earthquakes, all these are the Beginning of sorrows. Jesus said for us to watch for ye know not what hour your Lord doth come. He could come before night. Will you be ready? I'm going to wait until things in the world get better. The conditions will become worse and worse and then suddenly the Lord will come. John looked up, the door was opened in heaven and the voice of Jesus cried come up hither, John representing the true church, not a building but a true body of people that come together to service him.

(2 Cor. 5:21) When we trust in Christ, we make an exchange He take our sin and make us right with God. Our sins were laid on Christ at his Crucifixion. God offers to trade His righteousness for our sins. He offers salvation to all people many people put off a decision for Christ,

thinking that there will be a better time. They could easily miss their opportunity altogether don't go to sleep on Jesus he is waiting the door is open. He is waiting for you, you, and you to come to him.

There is no time like the present to receive, and ask Jesus forgiveness, don't let anything hold you back from coming to Christ Jesus. If you don't know Jesus Christ as your Lord and Savior it is time to get to know him. (vs.7) and the first beast was like a lion and the second beast like a calf, and the third beast had a face as a man, and the fourth beast was like a flying eagle. These beasts are not real animals, they are the highest order of angels. That guard God's throne. They lead others in worship, God symbolized in the animal like appearance of these four beings are majesty and power the lion, faithfulness, (the calf) intelligence the man. (vs. 8) And the four beasts had each of them six wings about him and they were full of eyes with in, and they rest not day and night saying, Holy, Holy, Holy, Lord God almighty which was and is to come.

A door is an opening through which we pass from one room to another from one place to another. The scripture tells us that there is one door into heaven Jesus is the door by me if any man come enter he shall be saved. Jesus is the door. He is the way into heaven those who come by faith he shuts in. The one who can't open the door, those who reject him he shuts out in darkness. In other word they will go to Hell if you have not let Jesus in your life into your heart, open your door let Him come in. No one is good enough to save him or herself if we want to live eternal with Christ we must depend totally on God grace.

Many people believe that to survive in the world a person must be tough and strong. God says not by might, nor by power, but by my spirit. When we live for God we cannot trust in our own strength or our abilities. Instead, depend on God and work in the power of his spirit. After a brief period of great tribulation, the Lord will return to this earth to set up His kingdom, and at the manifestation of Christ and the saints the entire creation will be redeemed. When Christ died on Calvary He died not only to save us from going to hell. He saved us to live with Him on the earth (Rev.6:5) And when he had open, the third seal, I heard the third beast say come and see. And I beheld and lo a black horse and he that sat on him had a pair of balances in his hand. (vs.6) And I heard a voice in the midst of the four beasts say. A measure of wheat for a penny and three measures of barley for a penny and see thou hurt not the oil and the wine.

This black horse will bring starvation, people crops will be damage, contaminated water supplies, livestock will be destroyed. The only food will be for the army all caused by war, a day wages might buy one loaf of bread. The famine will be so great, food will be weighed by the oz. (Galatians 6:7) Be not deceived God is Not mocked for whatsoever a man soweth that shall he also reap. Famines will increase at a time just prior to Jesus return, why all this is happen that does not seen like God love us, God is allowing man to reap what he or she sows so that mankind will learn the bitter lesson that sin brings pain I have told you.

God said I will send pestilence among you, and you shall be given over to the enemy. Jesus Christ predicted this condition when he said and there shall be famines. But he meant more we have not seen anything hope we be gone on to heaven when this happen. This great famine will spread to all people, and nations of the earth until mankind turns to God in total surrender, God is teaching obedience.

God is allowing man to reap what he sows sin brings pain. Lot of people think I am doing this in the dark, no one will ever know it, but God know and sees everything we do. And here everything we say, He knows our every thought he knows what we are going to say before we say it, what a mighty God we serve. (Galatians 6:7) Be not deceived God is not mocked for whatsoever a man soweth that shall he also reap. (Rev.6:6) And I heard a voice in the midst of the four beasts say, a measure of wheat for a penny and three measures of barley for a penny, and see thou hurt not the oil and the wine. This black horse will bring starvation. God said I will send pestilence among you and you shall be given over to the enemy. (Leviticus 26:29) Instead of meat you shall eat your sons and daughters. Jesus Christ predicted this condition when he said, and there shall be famines, more than you ever seem.

This great famine will spread to all people. And nations of the earth until mankind turns to God total surrender. God is teaching man obedience, he is allowing man to reap what he sows, (Rev.8) And I looked and behold a pale horse and his name that sat on him was Death and Hell followed with him, and power was given unto them over the fourth part of the earth, to kill with sword and with hunger and with death and with the beasts of the earth. The four horsemen are given control of one fourth of the earth, indicating that God is still limiting his judgment, meaning it is not yet complete.

With these Judgments there is still time for people to turn to Christ and away from sin, in this case the limited punishment not only demonstrates God's wrath on sin but also his merciful love in giving people yet another opportunity to turn to him before he brings final judgment.

This fourth horseman, he will bring a worldwide disease and millions more will die. Somebody thinking while God is so mean God is not mean, he is a just God, he have told you in his word how to live. He is telling you what will happen in the last days, he will send pestilence all kind of disease. God tells you in (Lev.26:29) I will also send wild beasts among you, which shall rob you of your children and destroy your cattle. Instead of the animals' blood at the foot of the alter John saw the souls who had died or been kill for preaching God's Word.

The four horsemen are given control of one fourth of the earth, indicating that God is still limiting his judgment. Meaning it is not yet complete with the judgments there is still time for people to turn to Christ and away from sin. In this case the limited punishment not only demonstrates God's wrath on sin but also his merciful love in giving people yet another opportunity to turn to him before he brings final judgment. This fourth horseman, will bring a worldwide disease and millions more will die. Somebody thinking while God is so mean God is not mean, He is a just God, he have told us in his word how to live, he is telling us what will happen in the last days, he will send pestilence all kind of disease. I have told you twice get ready.

They are eager for God to bring justice to the earth. But they are told to wait, we want justice immediately we must be patient God work on his own time table and he promises justice.

(Rev. 6:12) And I beheld when he had opened the sixth seal and low there was a great earthquake and the sun become black as sackcloth of hair and the moon become as blood. Jesus talked about that in (Matt 24:29. Everyone will be afraid when the earth itself trembles, suddenly they realize who Jesus is, but it is too late they have rejected him (Rev. 6:16) and said to the mountain and rocks fall on us and hide us from the face of him that sitteth on the throne and from the wrath of the Lamb. (Rev. 6:17) For the great day of his wrath is come and who shall be able to stand.

At the sight if God sitting on the throne all human beings great and small will be terrified calling for the mountains to fall on them so they will not have to face the judgment of the lamb. For the great day of his wrath is come and who shall be able to stand. The answer to that is no one the thing we must do is make sure that we are not left here to face all of these horrors. How do we do that by selling out to Jesus now make him Lord of your life now before it is too late.

Revelation is written to the church, the Christians it encourages us to look forward to heaven. It also tells us the terrible things we will be saved from when the wrath descends on this earth. It leads true Christians to their friends and family while there is still time knowing what is coming, we certainly don't want to leave anyone behind.

When God put you on hold, don't hung up He may not come when you want Him to, but He is always on time, he is an on time God. Keep the Faith, keep on praying, whatever ever you might be going through just hold on, when God put you on hold don't give up. Hold on and keep praying. Take up your cross every day and following Jesus, are you willing to deny yourself by taking up your cross daily and follow him. Jesus promises a reward for those who have been faithful to him.

God allowed trouble to come to us in order to help us. Our troubles can be helpful because they can humble us. Troubles will make us more faithful to God make us more dependent upon God. When you are going through the battle of life give God thanks because the battle is not yours it's the Lord. Committed yourself to the Lord invite the Lord to go with you God will protect you. Commit yourself to the Lord This is your time to be bless, let God be number one in your life, but Jesus committed himself to us are you committed today? If Jesus was not committed to you and I we would not be here. Following Jesus meant a true commitment when you run into a wall don't know what to do. Don't turn back Jesus got your back he did not say he would come when you want him to.

(Matt. 9:28) The bind men were persistent they went right into the house where Jesus was staying. They were committed, they knew Jesus could heal them they would not let nothing stop them from finding him that's faith. (Matt. 6:30) Wherefore, if God so clothe the grass of the field, which today is, and tomorrow is cast into the oven, shall he not much more clothe you, O ye of little faith? When we believe God's word in our heart and we pray in line with His Word, you have every right to expect your prayer to bring results. They knocked a hole in the roof and lowered him into the room on a stretcher. The owner of that house thought as much of his roof as you think of yours, how do you suppose he reacted when they tore a hole in his roof?

These men had one thing in mind: to reach Jesus. They put aside their own dignity and refuse to fear the owner of the house or the people around them. When they lowered the sick man into the room, (Luke 5:20) say that Jesus **SAW THEIR FAITH.** The invisible force of faith because visible through their action! In response to faith, Jesus forgave the man's sins and healed his body.

Prayer, at its best, is a process of training the universe to be a good employee. In addition, it is training oneself to be an employer worthy of the universe's trust. After all, the trick is allowing oneself to make a clean decision. It is hard to do that if one thinks of oneself as evil and destructive. Most of us, all the time, think this will happen immediately, in addition some think "no, it won't" we do not trust ourselves. Therefore, there is much to learn about making decisions and having them work out.

God is just waiting for you to talk to Him, waiting just for those few brief moments when you acknowledge him, think about him, and show him some love and respect. Yes your God is just waiting for you to talk to him and he desperately wants to talk to you, not in words, but through your mind and your heart. God is going to pass the vocal cords and the ear and instead your heart will feel that gentle tugging, that urging, that pulling. Your heart and mind will know exactly what God is trying to tell you. You have to begin to communicate with God and listen for God to speak, you have to get your heart in the right condition.

God want each believer to know what he expects from them, and what each believer can expect from God. Jesus was speaking to all believers down through all the ages. (James 5:15) And the prayer of faith shall save the sick and the Lord shall raise him up; and if he have committed sins. They shall be forgiven him. I pray, but I am still, going through. So many times God will wait, but remember he come on his on time. Some time he will just wait, while you are waiting on him, he is teaching you faith, understanding, how to believe and truth him, don't give up just hold on wait on Jesus. Be patient, trust God to do what he promises. God is not slack concerning his promises.

You can pray, and pray God still come on his on time table. I cry and I pray, but David said weeping may in due for a night, but wait on the Lord, Joy cometh in the morning. God want us to give him his proper place in our life. Don't put him on the back, and when you need him run and get him, it will not work that way.

(Mark 11:22-24) And Jesus answering saith into them, have faith in God. For verily I say unto you, that whosoever shall say unto this mountain, be thou removed, and be thou cast into the sea; and shall not doubt in his heart, but shall believe that those things which he saith shall come to pass; he shall have whatsoever he saith; Therefore, I say unto you, what things so ever ye desire, when ye pray, believe that ye receive them, and ye shall have them.

The first step in praying a pray of faith is qualify your desire. Make sure that you want to release faith lines up with the word of God. Second, ask for what you desire according to the word of God

CHAPTER 3

THE LAMB OF GOD

Let us look at this passage of scripture I believe that the one thing that holds our attention in this book. Is that John couldn't open the book in this scripture. It is really challenging us, it is challenging us to rise to a new level another level so that we will be able to see what his power is all about we will be able to know what the future holds. This is the only book in the Bible that promises a blessing to those who listen to its word and do what it says.

It was to be sealed and preserved to give people in the end times the needed hope that God will ultimately conquer all evil, Daniels did not understand the exact meaning of the times and events in his vision. We can see events as they unfold we are in the end times. (Rev. 22:10) and he saith unto me seal not the saying of the prophecy of this book for the time is at hand. The angel tells John what to do after his vision is over Daniels was commanded to seal up his book.

John Book is left open so that all can read and understand, Daniel's massage was sealed because it was not a massage for Daniels's time, but the book of Revelation was a message for John's time and for you and I. My brothers and sisters Christ's return is getting closer (vs 5) and one of the elders saith unto me weep not, behold the Lion of the tribe of Judah the Root of David hath prevailed to open the book and loose the seven seals thereof. Jesus conquered sin death, hell, and

Satan himself, couldn't nobody do that but Jesus only Jesus can be trusted with the world's future.

The root of David refute to Jesus being from David's family line. Jesus is picture as both a Lion and a Lamb. The Lion symbolizing his authority and power. The Lamb symbolizing his submission to God's will. Christ the Lamb was the perfect sacrifice for the sins of all mankind only Christ can save us from terrible events revealed by the scroll It's not your Battle.

We may not fight an enemy army, but every day we battle temptation, pressure, rulers of the darkness of the world. We have God spirit in us if we ask for God's help when we face struggles. God will fight for you and I, and always win. How do we let God fight for us? We got to realize that the battle is not ours it is God battle.

God already told his children in his word that He would fight our battle. The word said that the battle is not your, it belongs to the Lord. In the midst of the battle we must know that the Lord is working things out for you. We as Christians know that the Devil goes about as a roaring lion seeking whom he may devour. Everybody that say Lord, Lord is not save, when you are living according to the Word, you can get bold with that old Devil. Demand that he leaves you alone in the name of Jesus.

Jesus already whipped him, so you can put him on the run with the name of Jesus stay in contact with people who are filled with God's spirit. Before David went to battle he prayed to God, asking for his presence and guidance. Too often we wait until we are in trouble before turning to God.

God didn't leave you without help or comfort in this life, Jesus himself promised to give you grace in every situation. His grace is sufficient to sustain you through every problem and trials he also promised you the victory in every situation. Standing in faith on God's word is how you fight the good fight of faith we have to many people fighting one another, stop and let God fight your battle. Some believers have the idea that they'll never have a battle, they'll never have a struggle they will never have any problems in this life. (Hosea Ch4:6) My people are destroyed for lack of knowledge. Just because people are members of a church or hear a message on faith or listen to teaching tapes, is no sign they have bible knowledge, they can hear but may not receive.

Or they can hear with their mind but not with their heart or sometimes what they hear confuses them WHY? Because they have not developed a relationship with God. The lack of knowledge cause faith to perish It's sad when believers are more concerned with getting than they with giving. (John Ch 3:16) Tells us God so loved the world that he gave his only son, in other words God motive was to give and love renew your mind with the promises of God, always remember this is not your battle. For example the word of God has already told you that by His stripes you are healed. It doesn't say you are going to be healed it say you are already healed. When we service him, the word promises that God shall supply all of your needs according to His riches in glory. Jesus heals Peter mother –in-law he is still in the healing business, He heal a man with leprosy a paralyzed man. The battle is not your, it the LORD, In the Christian life we battle against principalities and power the powerful evil forces of fallen angels headed by Satan. We as Christian have got to withstand Satan attacks, we must depend on God strength and use every piece of his armor. There are real Demons Satan has control, we face a powerful army his goal is to defeat Christ Jesus. We will struggle in this world until Jesus comes because Satan is constantly battling against all who are on the Lord side we are engaged in a spiritual battle because we are no longer on the Satan side. Paul tells us use every piece of God's armor to resist Satan's attacks and to stand true to God in the midst of Satan attacks.

We are not told to fight the Devil, we are told that God will fight for us, Sometime God will let your enemy help you grow (Ephesian Ch

6) Paul talked about being a soldier on the Battle field. The church is a soldier, we have too many people in the church have pull their armor off they are relight. Paul said be strong in the Lord in the power of his might, put on the armor of God in order that ye may be able to stand.

Many churches have lost sight of the spiritual battle we feel that if we have a lovely church building and attracting crowds, good finances are coming in everything is fine. The battle are the word of God being taught, the few that is left are they getting the word. Is there a spirit of love and cooperation among your members? is there a spirit of criticism and bitterness? hate in your church, some people come to church when they are ready, they only come to make trouble God is not the Arthur of confusion. It is easy to say we love the Lord when it doesn't cost us anything maybe go to church once a month.

The real test of our love for God is how we treat one other we cannot truly love God while neglecting to love one another. The Devil is very real originally he was an angel of God, but through his pride he became corrupt. Satan is God's enemy he constantly tries to hinder God's work. But he is limited by God power. He can do only what God permitted him to do. He looks for spiritually weak people who think they are better than other. You have got to know who you are in Christ Jesus then you can do what you are called to do. Check your armor because God is able to do exceedingly abundantly above all that we ask or think. According to the power that works in us, the power of the Holy Spirit taking the shield of faith, so you will quench all the fiery darts of the wicked. Take the helmet of salvation and the sword of the spirit, which is the word of GOD.

It seems like sometime your armor is falling off just hold on keep the faith. You may have been through the storm of life but hold on' God did not say it would be easy but hold on keep the faith. In the storms, in our suffering that is when he takes us in his strong arms and carry us through. Have you ever been in a storm of life sometime storm after storm, but some time it take trials and tribulations to keep us humble. It take trials to keep us on our knees, we need to consider one important thing I believe He would want you to know. How could David get such a clear message from God? He may have prayed and been urged to action by the Holy Spirit. He may have asked God a Priest all our needs is God, and many hardship come with having God and he is enough. God is creator, He is Lord our savior and our deliver. God sent His angels to protect you from physical and spiritual harm.

There is a song that say It all day and night the angles keep watching over me. Let us remember, that God loves us and he is in control. We should not fret or worry Instead we should trust in the Lord. Give yourself to God for His use and safekeeping. We can't keep our self when we dwell on our problem, we will become anxious and angry. But God want us to concentrate on His goodness.

Out of all David went through he kept a humble attitude, when you dwell on your problems you will become anxious. They will be so terrified until they will be calling for the mountains to fall on them so they will not have to face the judgment of the Lamb. Now this word is not to frighten believers the believers will be with Jesus, all the VIP that showed no fear. No one who has rejected God can serve the day of his wrath but all those who belong to Christ will receives a reward. If there is a person sitting next to you while reading this book, just ask that person do you belong to Christ if so you need not fear these final days. (1 John 5:13) These things have I written unto you that believe on the name of the Son of God; that ye may know that ye have eternal life, and that ye may believe on the name of the Son of God.

Some people hope they will receive eternal life. John says we can know we have it. Our certainty is based on God's promise that he has given us eternal life through his Son. (Revelation 5:1-14)

(Mark 11:22-24) And Jesus answering saith unto them, Have faith in God. For verily I say unto you, that whosoever shall say unto this mountain. Be thou removed, and be thou cast into the sea; and shall not doubt in his heart, but shall believe that those things which he saith shall come to pass; he shall have whatsoever he saith. Therefore I say unto you, what things so ever ye desire, when ye pray, believe that ye receive them, and ye shall have them. The kind of prayer that moves mountains is prayer for the fruitfulness of God's Kingdom. It would seem impossible to move a mountain into the sea, so Jesus used that picture to show that God can do anything. God will answer your prayers, but not as a result of your positive mental attitude. (1) must be a believer; (2) you must not hold a grudge against another person; (3) you must not pray with selfish motives; (4) your request must be for the good of his Kingdom.

To pray effectively, you need faith in God, not faith in the object of your request. If you focus only on your request, you will be left with nothing if your request is refused. "All things are possible unto thee; not what I will, but what thou wilt" Our prayers are often motivated by our own interests and desires. We like to hear that we can have anything. But Jesus prayed with God's interests in mind. When we pray, we can express our desire, but we should want his will above ours. Check yourself to see if your prayers focus on your interests or God's.

Confess the Word of God over your situation no matter what it looks like around you. Do everything in the realm of your influence that you can in agreement with what you asked God do. Faith pleases God, and God rewards those who diligently seek Him by faith. All of the promises are received by faith. We will overcome every situation and circumstance by faith. Faith is not something that you use when you need it. Faith is a life style, (Romans 1:17) states the just shall live by faith.

We Christians believe that the prayer of Jesus teaches that prayer is always heard, in his prayer is our hope. What can we learn from the prayer of Jesus? First, that true prayer should come from the heart.

He prayed from within, not with just words or gestures. His prayer was not based only on feeling or passing emotions, prayer come from within, beyond level of feelings, from us. "Go into the inner room," "Jesus says, and there pray to your Father, who hears you."

Sometime pray from the heart, from the "inner room" takes the form of words, at other times it may be like his wordless cry. Secondly, Prayer is fed by faith. Jesus prayed with an unwavering faith in his heavenly Father, a faith that lasted until his death. He taught us to pray also with childlike faith in God, believing that the one who loves us hears our prayers.

Thirdly, prayer should be steady and persevering as his prayer was even when no answer comes or when no relief is in sight. "Watch and Pray." "He says, seek and knock," until the door that reveals God's Holy's will be opened. The disciples asked Jesus to teach them to pray. He did, and he teaches us too. He answered by teaching them the prayer we call, Our Father or the Lord's Prayer. The Lord's Prayer is a Christian prayer. The Lord's Prayer is a basic Christian prayer, every Christian learn it by heart.

By calling God "Father," we are more rightly describing ourselves and our relationship with God. Jesus teaches that we have a filial relationship with God; God sees us as if we were a daughter or a son. Thy Kingdom come, thy will be done, on earth as it is in heaven. God's kingdom, Jesus often said that God's power would appear and renew all creation. God like a mighty king would rule over the earth according to a plan that unfolds from the beginning of the world. Peace and justice would mark God's kingdom. Good would be rewarded and evil punished. The kingdom, according to Jesus, is not far off, but already present in our midst, though not yet revealed.

In the Lord's Prayer we pray that God's kingdom come that God's will, which is for our good, be done on earth as it is in heaven. Give us this day our daily bread. We are God's children. What can be more childlike than a petition in which we pray for our daily bread, a word that describes all those physical, human and spiritual gifts we need to live, with the confidence of children, we say, "Give us this day what we need." Forgive us our trespasses, as we forgive those who trespass against us. This petition of the Lord's prayer is a demanding one not only do we ask God's forgiveness for our daily offenses, but we link God's forgiveness of us with our forgiveness of others. Forgiving others is not always easy to do. We need God's help to do it. Nevertheless, it must be done or we ourselves cannot receive God's mercy.

In addition, lead us not into temptation, but deliver us from evil, Amen. Life is not easy, it is a daily battle. Trials like sickness and failure can crush our spirits. False values and easy promises can entice us and even destroy our souls. Therefore, we ask God to keep us from failing when we are tested, to help us to know the right thing to do, deliver us from the evil which awaits us in life.

The Lord's Prayer sums up the teaching of Jesus. It is also a prayer that offers the grace of Jesus. It is also a prayer that offers the grace of Jesus: his reverence got God, his childlike confidence in his Father, and his power to go bravely through life no matter what comes. When we pray his prayer, his spirit becomes our own. Yet Jesus is more than a teacher. As Christians we believe that Jesus prays for us; he is our intercessor before God. As Savior, he gathers our prayers, our needs, and the cries of our hearts to make them his own and offers them to God who hears our prayers in the prayer of his Son.

That is why we complete our prayers so often with the beautiful phrase: "Through Jesus Christ, our Lord. Amen." Jesus is our teacher and he is our Savior, who takes out prayers and makes them his own. We learn about the attributes of God by analyzing the prayers of people in the bible. For instance, when Daniel knelt to pray, he knowingly violated a civil code that required he only pray to a king proclaimed god. From Daniel's prayer, we learn that God is the highest God, and there are no other gods above Him. Ye shall not go after gods, of the gods of the people which are round about you; (For the Lord God is a jealous God among you. Lest the anger of the Lord thy God is kindled against thee, and destroy thee from off the face of the earth.

Many other prayers in the Bible show us the character of God and help us know him more intimately. I began pondering, "what would someone think about God if they listened to me pray." Would they see him as trustworthy? Would they see that he is pure, holy and powerful? (James4:8) tells us to drew nigh to God, and he will draw to you. Cleanse your hands, ye sinners; and purify your hearts, ye double minded. Someone ask the question? How can you draw close ("nigh") to God? (1)"submit to God" Realize that you need his forgiveness, and be willing to follow him. (2) "Resist the devil" don't allow him to tempt you. (3) "Cleanse your hands and purify your hearts." Be cleansed from sin, replacing it with God's purity (4) Let there be tears, sorrow, and sincere grief for your sins. Don't be afraid to express deep heartfelt for them. (5) Humble yourself before God, and he will lift you up.

(Jeremiah 33:3) Call unto me, and I will answer thee, and shew thee great and mighty things, which thou know not. God assures Jeramiah that he has only to ask. The same thing for you and I, He is ready to answer our prayers but we must ask for his assistance. Surely he could take care of our needs without our asking. But we must ask, we are acknowledging that he alone is God and that we cannot accomplish in our own strength all that is his domain to do. When we ask, we must humble ourselves, lay aside our willfulness and worry, and determine to obey him. Through prayer, we are able to be closer to almighty God than to anyone or anything else on this earth! This is an amazing and humbling gift.

Sha'drach, Me'shach, and A-bed'nego were young witnesses to the awesome power of prayer. When faced with the fate of being thrown into a fiery furnace or bow down to King Nebuchadnezzar they chose the fiery furnace because they strongly believed in God and prayer. If it be so, our God whom we serve is able to deliver us from the burning fiery furnace, and he will deliver us out of thine hand, O king. Through their faith and belief in God, when He heard they call He delivered them and King Nebuchadnezzar became a believer and honored God.

(Daniel3:12) There are certain Jews whom thou hast set over the affairs of the province of Babylon, Shadrach, Meshach, and Abednego; these men, O king, have not regarded thee: they serve not thy gods, nor worship the golden image which thou hast set up. Why didn't the three men just bow to the image and tell God that they didn't mean it? They had determined never to worship another god, and they courageously took their stand. As a result, they were condemned and led away to be executed. They did not know whether they would be delivered from the fire; all they knew was that they would not bow to an idol.

Are you ready to take a stand for God no matter what? When you stand for God, you will stand out. It may be painful, and it may not always have a happy ending. Be prepared to say, "If he delivers me, or if he doesn't, I will serve only God."

(Psalm 20:1-4) The Lord hear thee in the day of trouble; the name of the God of Jacob defend three; Send thee help form the sanctuary, and strengthen thee out of Zion; Remember all thy offerings, and accept thy burnt sacrifice; Selah. Grant thee according to thine own heart, and fulfil all thy counsel. Pray for victory in the battle, pray can help us prepare for any great challenge, just pray and stand still and let God fight the battle, all our trust should be placed in the Lord he has all power, we have a little power.

A good leader must trust God and depends upon his steadfast love, keep the Lord God at the center of your life and depend on him. His love will keep you from stumbling. When we trust God, we have permanence and stability. We may have to cry sometime, even have pain in the body sometime we may lose a great deal, we may be hurts, but we cannot be moved out of God's favor. He will be our foundation that solid rock. He will never leave or desert us, He is our father.

(Lamentations 3:23-24) They are new every morning great is thy faithfulness. The LORD is my portion, my soul; therefore will I hope in him. Jeremiah knew from personal experience about God's faithfulness. God had promised that punishment would follow disobedience, and it did. But God also had promised future restoration and blessing, and Jeremiah knew that God would keep that promise also. Trusting in God's faithfulness day by day makes us confident in his great promises for the future.

(James 5:14-15) Is any sick among you? Let him call for the elders of the church; and let them pray over him, anointing him with oil in the name of the Lord: and the prayer of faith shall save the sick, and the Lord shall raise him up; and if he has committed sins, they shall be forgiven him. People in the church are not alone. Members of Christ's body should be able to count on others for support and prayer, especially when they are sick or suffering. The elders should be on call to respond to the illness of any member, and the church should stay alert to pray for the needs of all its members.

"The prayer of faith" does not refer to the faith of the sick person, but to the faith of the people praying. God heals, faith doesn't and all prayers are subject to God's will. But our prayers are part of God's healing process.

(And it came to pass, when I heard these words, that I sat down and wept, and mourned certain days, and fasted, and prayed before the God of heaven, and beseech thee. O LORD God of heaven, the great and terrible God, that keepeth covenant and mercy for them that love him and observe his commandment: let thine ear now be attentive, and thine eyes open, that thou mayest hear the prayer of thy servant which I pray before thee now, day and night, for the children of Israel thy servants and confess the sins of the children of Israel, which we have sinned against thee: both I and my father's house have sinned.

Nehemiah was a good example of a prayer warrior, we can learn about how to pray from him. The book of Nehemiah tells about how Nehemiah got bad news from the city of Jerusalem. The city Jerusalem had been rebuilt after enemies had destroycd it, but the walls around the city had never been rebuilt and were lying in pieces. They greatly upset Nehemiah. He prayed, pay attention to what he did before he prayed and to how he prayed.

He sat down and wept, and mourned certain days, and fasted before he began to pray. In verses 5 and 7 he praised God, confessed sins, and asked forgiveness. When he said, "I beseech thee, O LORD of heaven, the great and terrible God, that keepnet covenant and mercy for them that love him and observe his commandments: Let thine eat now be attentive, and thine eyes open, that thou mayest hear the prayer of thy servant, which I pray before thee now, day and night, for the children of Israel thy servants, and confess the sins of the children of Israel, which we have sinned against thee: both I and my father's house have sinned.

We have dealt very corruptly against thee, and have not kept the commandments, nor the statutes, nor the judgment, which thou commanded thy servant Moses." (He asked forgiveness on the behalf of others." Verses 8-9 show he had been reading Gods Word. In Nehemiah 2:4, he prayed a quick prayer while talking to the King. I would guess he prayed for the right words to use to convince the king and that the king would allow Nehemiah to rebuild the wall. Notice he prayed while he was talking to the King. It appears he may have been in constant communication with God. Maybe he was "abiding" in God the way Jesus said in John 15:7, "If ye abide in me, and my words abide in you, ye shall ask what ye will, and it shall be done unto you.'

In Nehemiah Ch.4:4-5 some enemies of Nehemiah were trying to make him stop building the wall. They were making fun of him and his work.

Instead of arguing with them or fighting with them, Nehemiah prayed about their behavior right then, he knew that pray changes things, the apostles knew the necessity and worth of prayer to their ministry. They knew that their high commission as apostles, instead of relieving them from the necessity of prayer, committed them to it by a more urgent need, so that they were exceedingly jealous else some other important work should exhaust their time and prevent their praying as they ought; so they appointed laymen to look after the delicate and engrossing duties of ministering to the poor, that they (the apostles) might unhindered, "give themselves continually to prayer and to the ministry of the word." Prayer is put first, and their relation to prayer is put most strongly—"give themselves to it," making a business of it, surrendering themselves to praying, putting fervor, urgency, perseverance, and time in it.

How holy, apostolic men devoted themselves to this divine work of prayer! "Night and day praying exceedingly," says Paul. "We will give ourselves continually to prayer" They prayed mightily day and night to bring their people to the highest regions of faith and holiness. They prayed mightier still to hold them to this high spiritual altitude. We should be mindful of the gift that our father in heaven gave to all of us. God loved us so much that he gave us his only Son, Jesus Christ. Though his Son never sinned despite being tempted as we all are. He died on the cross to pay the debt for our sins, and so that we could be with the father through Him. Then Jesus Christ rose again from the dead to show that once the debt of sin has been paid for, death has no power over a person, and that just as our sins could be forgiven we could overcome death with him. This is possible because Jesus Christ was the true Son of God, meaning that he is equal to God, is part of God, and is God. And the result of God giving up heaven for a time to come to earth and doing this, what no animal or man could, people need not receive the punishment for sins, but can everlasting life. This is also possible because God is eternal and all powerful, capable of doing whatever He sees fit. Well, God wanted and saw fit to save you from your sins, and He made a way possible, and that way was His Son Jesus Christ.

CHAPTER

PREPARING TO PRAY

"May the words of my mouth and the meditation of my heart be pleasing in your sight O Lord, my Rock and my Redeemer' (Psalms 19:14) To develop a lifestyle of prayer in our lives, we need to have that same calmness of you. To achieve that, we must first prepare our hearts and minds for prayer. We wouldn't think of going on a long car trip without checking the map to see where we're going, packing what we 'll need, and making sure our car is in working condition and has a full tank of gas. In the same way, we need to prepare ourselves for prayer. Our road map is God's Word we should study it to know God's promises and direction for our life.

A study of the meditative lifestyles of some believers reveals the ample time they set aside to live close to God and to listen to Him. To develop a lifestyle of prayer in our lives, we need to have that same calmness of spirit. **To achieve that, we must first prepare our hearts and minds for prayer. We should have no excess baggage on our trip,** which means we need to clear away any distractions so we can focus on aligning ourselves with our Redeemer in prayer. In addition, to make sure we are in working condition, we need to clean our thoughts, have the right attitude for prayer and have the right relationship with God and others.

Do not let this book of the Law depart from your mouth; meditate on it day and night, so that you may be careful to do everything written in it. Then you will be prosperous and successful (Joshua 1:8). The Word of God must permeate every aspect of our lives in order for us to be able to pray. In addition, God commands us, along with Joshua, to learn His Word and speak it in prayer to receive His blessings. By learning His Word, we learn about our Creator and Redeemer.

We know His will for us, His expectations for us, and His love and grace. We see Him more clearly, and we align our thoughts and wishes with His. God wants us to know Him in a personal relationship built through prayer. If we do those things without a close relationship with our Redeemer, we are not doing His will. God knows the desires of our heart. (Psalm 55:17) Praying morning noon, and night is certainly an excellent way to maintain correct priorities throughout every day. The prayers of God's people are effective against the overwhelming evil in the world, trusting in God's care in the midst of fear. When all seems dark, one truth still shines bright: When God is for us those against us will never succeed.

A prayer for God's Just, when no justice can be found, rejoice in knowing that justice will triumph because there is a God who will judge with complete fairness Listing to the word, **It's Praying Times**: Trusting in God's care in the midst of fear. When all seems dark, one truth still shines bright: When God is for you those against you will never succeed. God will never forsake those who trust in him. To forsake someone is to abandon that person, God's promise does not mean that if we trust in him we will escape less of suffering; it means that God himself will never leave us no matter what we face.

(1 Timothy 2 :8) I will therefore that men pray everywhere, lifting up holy hands, without wrath and doubting. Besides being displeasing to God, it is difficult to pray when we have sinned or when we feel angry and resentful. That why Jesus told us to interrupt worship. If necessary, to make peace with others. Our gold should be to have

a right relationship with God and also with others. Besides being displeasing to God, it is difficult to pray when we have sinned or when we feel angry and resentful. That is when Jesus' interrupt worship if worship told us to interrupt worship If necessary, to make peace with others. Our goal should be to have a right relationship with God and also with others.

Someone is thinking how we ought to pray Jesus emphasizes the sincerity of our heart. He does not want out empty words. We can pray silently, we can pray loud, we can pray in our own words or using the words of the scriptures. We can pray with the mind or we can pray with the spirit. Another method of praying is singing to the Lord (Psalm 92:1). It is a good thing to give thanks unto the Lord and to sing praises unto thy name. We must thank the Lord morning and evening for salvation through His Son Jesus for his lovingkindness, His grace, and for His faithful guidance and care. God made provision for us to receive anything we need in this life, but our desires have to be in line with His Word. We can't expect God to give us something that violates His Word. The (2 Kings 20:1-2) In those days was Hezekiah sick unto death. And the prophet Isaiah the son of Amos came to him, thus saith the LORD, set thine house in order; for thou shalt die, and not live Vs.2 Then he turned his face to the wall, and prayed unto the LORD, saying Vs.3 I, beseech thee, O LORD, remember now how I have walked before thee in truth and with a perfect heart, and have done that which is good in thy sight, and Hezekiah wept sore. And it came to pass, afore Isaiah was gone out gone out the middle court, that the word of the LORD came to him, saying, Vs.5 Turn again, and tell turn again, and tell Hezekiah the captain of my people, thus saith the LORD, the God of David thy father, I have heard thy prayer, I have seen thy tear behold, I will heal thee on the third day thou shalt go up unto the house of the LORD.

Although Hezekiah came boldly to God, he went to the Temple and prayed. God answered Hezekiah's prayer and delivered Judah by sending an angel to attack the Assyrian camp. Ahaz ignored Isaiah,

Hezekiah listened to his advice. To read prophecies, see the book of Isaiah. Hezekiah's prayer provides a good model for us. We should not be afraid to approach God with our prayers, but we must come to him with respect for who he is and what he can do.

(Psalm 5:1-2) Vs.1-2 Give ear to my words, O LORD, consider my meditation. Hearken unto the voice of my cry, my King, and my God for unto three will I pray.

The secret of a close relationship with God is to pray to him earnestly in the morning. In the morning, our minds are freer from problems, and then we can commit the whole day to God. Regular communication helps any friendship and is certainly necessary for a strong relationship with God. We need to communicate with him daily. Do you have a regular time to pray and read God's Word? 1 John 5:13 and 14.[th]These things have I written unto you believe on the name of the Son of God; that ye may know that ye have eternal life, and that ye may believe on the of God. 14th And this is the confidence that we have in him, that, if we ask any thing according to his will, he heareth us: (15vs.) and if we know that he hear us, whatever we ask, we know that we have the petitions that we desired of them.

Some people hope they will receive eternal life. John says we can know we have it. Our certainty is based on God's promise that he has given us eternal life through his Son. This is true whether you feel close to God or distant from him. Eternal life is not based on feelings but on facts. You can know you have eternal life if you believe God's truth. If you aren't sure that you are a Christian, ask yourself: "Have I honestly committed my life to him as my Savior and Lord?" If so, you know by faith that you are indeed a child of God.

The emphasis here is on God's will not our will. When we communicate with God, we don't demand what we want: rather we discuss with him what he wants for us. If we align our prayers to his will, he will listen; and we can be certain that if he listens, he will give us a definite answer. God's word is his will, when you pray in line with the word, you have automatically prayed in line with God's will clearly be heard by the Father. After you pray and receive your salvation by faith, you then simply thank God for it.

During His time on earth, Jesus was the express image of God (Hebrews 1:3). What did He do? He healed the sick, (Acts 10:38) God anointed Jesus of Nazareth with the Holy Ghost and power: who went about doing good and heading all that were oppressed of the Devil; for God was with him. The prayer for healing is a simple one. "Father in the name of Jesus I see in your Word that healing belongs to me. I believe it, I receive it. I thank you for it. I act upon it now. Once you have prayed, TRUST God, have FAITH,

When you pray, all you have to do is apply your faith. Where does faith come from? How do you get faith? Faith come by hearing and hearing by the Word of God. Once you have prayed in faith, hold fast to your confession. God is aware of your situation. His power went to work the instant you prayed in faith. A very misunderstood concept throughout the religious world is that it is extremely difficult to get God to answer prayer at all -much less answer all prayers. That is a lie of Satan and absolutely contrary to the Word to God. When you believe God's Word in your heart and you pray in line with His Word, you have every right to expect your prayer to bring results. Jesus said: "Verily I say unto you, if ye have faith, and doubt not ye shall not only do this which is done to the fig tree, but also if ye shall say unto this mountain, be thou removed, and be thou cast into the sea; it shall be done. And all things, whatsoever ye shall ask in prayer, believing, ye shall receive" (Matthew 21:21-22).

If God answer the prayer of a sinner to be saved, He will certainly answer the prayers of born-again believers who come to him in faith concerning their lives. Satan uses doubt with great skill and cunning to cause you to fail. He knows the importance of getting you to waver. He constantly tries to throw doubt and unbelief into your consciousness. God is on our side! Prepare to succeed, not to fail. When you pray in Jesus' Name, according to the Word in Faith, God will quickly respond to you (John 16:23).

Suppose you prayed for healing. Then you think, what will I do if God does not heal me? Maybe I had better get an appointment with the doctor. He is very busy this time of year. I might not be able to see him. Then if God does not heal me, I will be in a mass! With that attitude, believing God will be a waste of time. Prayer, at its best, is a process of training the universe to be a good employee. In addition, it is training oneself to be an employer worthy of the universe's trust. After all, the trick is allowing oneself to make a clean decision. It is hard to do that if one thinks of oneself as evil and destructive. Most of us, most of the time, think this will happen immediately. In addition, some think, "No, it won't." We do not trust ourselves. Therefore, there is much to learn about making decisions and having them work out.

There may be faster surer ways then prayer to learn this, but prayer can help. To learn to trust ourselves, we align ourselves with that in which we trust. God is just waiting for you to talk to Him, waiting just for those few brief moments when you acknowledge him, think about him, and show him some love and respect. Yes, your God is just waiting for you to talk to him and he desperately wants to talk to you, not in words but through your mind and your heart. God is going to pass the vocal cords and the ear and instead your heart will feel that gentle tugging, that pulling. Your heart and mind will know exactly what God is trying to tell you.

Sometimes it seem like God does not hear us when we pray, but don't give up, keep praying keep the faith, believe and trust Him, never give up on Jesus, He didn't give up on you, so don't you give on him. If we line up with God's word, pray in faith, believe and go on and thank God for whatever you ask him for. Believing it is done.

You have to learn how to speak to your problems. When you pray do not have doubt in your heart, we have got to believe that it is done. Jesus tells us in Mark 11:24, "Therefore I say to you, whatever things you ask when you pray, believe that you receive them, and you will have them. Many times just before God blesses us, He will stand back, and let the Devil put a mountain in our life. Just to see if we can come through without doubting. There is no peace without the grace of God, and there is no grace of God without prayer." It is a conversation of the heart with God. Prayer is a cleaning process, washing our thoughts, feelings motives, and will, purifying the entire being including the heart, thus enabling us to see God, for without purity no one can see God.

Prayer is what you do when you are done struggling with a problem, and you are ready to call forth its solution. It is about allowing God to do something through you. We Christians learn to pray through Jesus Christ, who not only teaches us to pray, but also prayed himself. His prayer filled the gospels. Did Jesus himself have to learn to pray? Yes, he did he was the son of God who knew all things. Even in his earliest years, Jesus prayed to God with a distinct intimacy. God was his father and he was God's son. Jesus prayed regularly his first disciples recalled. He prayed before decisive moments, beginning with his baptism and as he faced his passion and death, He prayed in times of human weakness and death, as he did at the grave of Lazarus.

His prayer was heartfelt, nowhere is that more evident than when he prayed on the cross. "Father, forgive them, for they know not what they do." "Woman, behold your son, son behold your mother." My God, my God why have you forsaken me? "It is finished;" Father, into your hands I commend my spirit." They were prayers that came from the heart. They reveal him tender towards those he loved and forgiving to those who wronged him: he is human in weakness and strong in faith. He ended his life with a loud cry. Even that last rending cry was a heartfelt prayer to God, issuing from the depths of his being and summing up what could not say. In addition, his prayer was heard. God raised him up.

We Christians believe the prayer of Jesus teaches that prayer is always heard, in his prayer is our hope. First, that true prayer should come from the heart. He prayed from within, not with just words of gestures. His prayer was not based only on feelings or passing emotions. Prayer comes from within, beyond level of feelings, "Go into the inner room, "Jesus says, "and there pray to your Father, who hears you." Sometime pray from the heart, from the "inner room" takes the form of words, at other times it may be like his wordless cry, Secondly. Pray is fed by faith. Jesus prayed with an unwavering faith in his heavenly Father, a faith that last until his death. He taught us to pray also with childlike in God, believing that the one who loves us hears our prayers. Thirdly, prayer should be steady and persevering as his prayer was even when no answer comes or when no relief is in sight. "Watch and Pray" he says, "Seek and knock," until the door that reveals God's Holy Will be opened.

The disciples asked Jesus to teach them to pray. He did, and he teaches us too. He answered by teaching them the prayer we call the Our Father or the Lord's Prayer. In the Lord's Prayer, Jesus invites us to draw near to God who is beyond human understanding, who dwells in mystery, who is all-holy. We can call God "Our Father" Thy Kingdom come, thy will be done, on earth as it is in heaven. God's kingdom, Jesus often said that God's power would appear and renew all creation. God like a mighty king would rule over the earth according to a plan that unfolds from the beginning of the world. Peace and justice would mark God's kingdom. Good would be rewarded and evil punished. The kingdom, according to Jesus is nor off but already present in our midst, though not yet revealed.

In the Lord's Prayer we pray that God's kingdom come that God's will which is for our good, be done on earth as it is in heaven. Give us this day our daily bread. We are God's children, what can be more childlike than a petition in which we pray for daily bread. We are God children. What can be more childlike than a petition in which we pray for our daily bread, a word that describes all those physical, human and spiritual gifts we need to live. With the confidence of children we say, "Give us this day what we need." Forgive us our trespasses, as we forgive those who trespass against us. This petition of the Lord's Prayer is a demanding one, not only do we ask God's forgiveness for our daily offenses, but also, we link God's forgiven us with our forgiven of others. Forgiving others is not always to do, we need God's help to do it nevertheless, it must be done or we ourselves cannot receive God's mercy.

In addition lead us not into temptation but deliver us from evil. Amen Life is not easy it is a daily battle, trials like sickness and failure can crush our spirits. False values and easy promises can entice us and even destroy our souls. Therefore, we ask God to keep us from failing when we are tested, to help us to know the right thing to do, to deliver us from evil, which waits us in life.

The Lord's Prayer sums up the teaching of Jesus, it is also a prayer that offers the grace of Jesus. It is also a prayer that offers the grace of Jesus; his reverence for God his childlike confidence in his power to go bravely through life no matter what comes. When we pray his prayer, his spirit becomes our own. Yet Jesus is more than a teacher, as Christians we believe that Jesus prays for us; he is our intercessor before God. As Savior, he gathers our prayers our needs and the cries of our hearts to make them his own and offers them to God who hears our prayers in the prayer of his Son.

That is why we complete our prayers so often with the beautiful phrase: "Through Jesus Christ, our Lord. Amen."

IT'S PRAYING TIME

The world supplication, we come to God in Prayer for many reasons, to worship him, to confess our sins and ask for forgiveness, to thank Him for his blessings. To ask for things for others so a prayer of supplication is asking God for something. In the New Testament (Matt. 6:11) Jesus tells us to ask for our daily bread, give us this day our daily bread.

(Luke 18:1-8) Jesus teaches us not to give up praying for what we need, not what we want but need. Prayers of supplication if there is no faith there is no need of praying, We have got to have faith that our prayers will be answer, when we began to pray Jesus the indwelling Holy Spirit on our behalf because we often don't know what or how to pray when we approach God. The spirit intercedes and prays for us it interpreter our supplication so when we are overwhelmed by trials and the cares of life, He assistance us with our prayers.

Have you ever been to the point you don't know the right words to pray, you open your mouth and nothing come out at this time the Holy Spirit prays with and for you, Paul say the spirit itself make intercession for us with groaning which cannot be uttered. Jesus told us to make peace with other we can't love God and hate our brother or our sister.

(1 John Ch 4 vs1) Beloved believe not every spirit but try the spirit whether they are of God: because many false prophets are gone out into the world. Vs.4 Ye are of God, little children, and have overcome them: greater is he that is in you, than he in that in the world.(1John Ch. 4 Vs 7 Beloved, let us love one another, for love is of God; and ever one that loveth is born of God, and know God.

Nothing sinful or evil can exist in God's presence, He is absolute goodness. He cannot overlook, condone or excuse sin as if it never happened. He loves us, but his love does not make him morally lax. If we trust in Jesus, however we do not have to bear the penalty for our sins. If no one has ever seen God, how can we ever know him? John in his Gospel said, "the begotten Son, which is the bosom of the Father, he hath declared him" (John 1:18). Jesus is the complete expression of God in human form he has revealed God to us. When we love one another, the invisible God reveal himself to others through us, and his love is made complete. It is easy to say we Love God when it doesn't cost us anything more than weekly attendance at religious services. But the real test of our love for God is how we treat the people right in front of us—our family members and fellow believers. We cannot truly love God while neglecting to love those who are created in his image.

(Ephesians Ch 6:18) Paul said praying always with all prayer and supplication in the spirit and watching there unto with all perseverance and supplication for all saints. If we suffer in the spirt is no easy path. Jesus suffered and we who follow him will also suffer.

It's Praying Time: Evening and morning and at noon will I pray and cry aloud, and he shall hear my voice. David said my heart is sore pained within me and the terrors of death are fallen upon me. (Psalm 55:6) And I said Oh that I had wings like a dove for then would I fly away and be at rest. David is telling us, I'm close to God I am man after his heart. But I have moments when I want to get away from it all and escape problems and pressures. It is when you are doing the best you can, and people just don't understand when you know it by God word. (Psalm 55:12) For it was not an enemy that reproached me, then I could have bear it. Neither was it he that hated me that did magnify himself against me then I would have hide myself from him.

Nothing hurts as much as a wound from a friend. He was in trouble he needed his friends. He was betrayal by a friend caused David great anguish, real friends stick by you in time of trouble, help you heal.

Job experience extreme physical pain as well as grief over the loss of his family, and his possessions. His friends came to see him to comfort and console him, there words of comfort were not helpful, God rebuked them for what they said.

Prayer is our best help when trials come our way because it keeps us in communion with God. David said evening and morning and at noon will I Pray and cry aloud and he shall hear my voice. It's praying time when evil come our way pray when sick in the body. It is very important to know what God word say, but it is much more important to obey his word. The Devil know the Word, he knows every word in the bible, but he can't live it. Do not forget that old Devil lives in heaven at one time.

(1 Peter 5:7) Casting all your care upon him for He care for you. Some people worry too much, give that problem to God. He is able to carry all of our worries and our struggles. Take it to the Lord in pray, Its praying time (Jonah 2Ch 1-4Vs.) Then Jonah prayed unto the Lord his God out of the fish's belly, And said, I cried by reason of mine affliction unto the LORD, and he heard me; out of the belly of hell cried I and thou hardest my voice. This is a Prayer of thanksgiving, not a prayer for deliverance. Jonah was simply thankful that he had not been drowned. He was delivered in a most spectacular way.

Jonah (Vs. 4) But it displeased Jonah exceedingly, and he was very angry. (Vs 2) And he prayed unto the Lord, and said, I pray thee, O

LORD, was not this my saying. God is slow to get angry, but when he is ready to punish, even the earth trembles. Often people avoid God because they see evildoers in the world and hypocrites in the church. They don't realize that because God is slow to anger, he gives his true followers time to share his love and truth with evildoers. But judgment will come.

To those who refuse to believe, God's punishment is like an angry fire. To those who love him, his mercy is security and peace, supplying all our needs diminishing his supply. But to his enemies he is a flood that will sweep them away. Anyone who remains arrogant and resists God's authority will face his anger. No ruler or nation will get away with rejecting him. No individual will be able to hide from his judgment. Those who keep trusting in God will be kept safe forever. No person on earth can safely defy God, the Almighty the Creator of all the universe. God, who controls the son, the galaxies, and the vest stretches beyond, also controls the rise and fall of nations. Some refuse to believe, God's punishment is like an angry fire to those who love him, his mercy is security and peace, supplying all our needs without diminishing his supply. But to his enemies he is a flood that will sweep them away. We can be confident that God's power and justice will one day conquer all evil. The LORD is good, a strong hold in the day of trouble; and he know them that trust in him. But with an overrunning flood he will make an utter end of the place thereof, and darkness shall pursue his enemies. No matter what happen, God is still in control of this world in spite of the apparent triumph of evil. God doesn't overlook sin.

Some Christians approach God with their heads hanging down, afraid to ask him to meet their needs. When you come to the throne of Grace, come boldly knowing that God will answer your prayer. God loves us, He loves us so much He sent Jesus to die for us, we can have eternal life through faith in him because he broke the power of death with his resurrection.

Through our battles and our trails God is still Good, when we don't understand and we ask the question why? God is still good. As we live for Jesus, we will experience the valley but Jesus promises to carry us through, He promise to be with us. He promises never to leave us. The sheep are completely dependent on the shepherd for provision guidance and protection.

David said even though I walk through the valley, the valley is not some where we stay our entire life. We walk through the valley. The valley is only temporary, He said his anger endure but a moment, in his favor is life weeping may endure for a night but joy cometh in the morning. Valley are going to happen only some are deeper than other, valleys happen throughout life sometime one right after another. It's not a matter of if I go in the valley, it's when I go in the valley.

We are going to have difficulty, disappointment, there will be times of suffering, sorrow, sickness, there will be times of frustration. Valleys come suddenly they are unpredictable, have you noticed how easily a good day can become a bad day. (Matthew 5:45) It rains on the just and the unjust. This is not heaven things are not perfect here, there are going to be some valleys. They are temporary it's not a permanent location. If we did not go through the valley somebody would never meet Jesus. If you never call on Jesus, in the valley you will call on him. It not if I go in the Valley it is when I go, you can fine victory in the valley, peace and Joy, you can fine Jesus, because He is the Lilly of the valley. He is the bright and morning star. God created Israel and made them special and called them by name. He protected them in times of trouble. We are important to God because we are his children. When we bear his wonderful name when we say that we know him as our savior.

(Isaiah 43:18-19) God created Israel and made them special to him. He redeemed them and called them by name, he protected them in time of trouble. We are important to God because we are his children. When we bear his wonderful name when we say that we know him as our savior. (Isaiah 43:2) When thou Passes through the water, I will be with thee, and through the river they shall not overflow thee. When thou walk through the fire thou shalt not be burned, neither shall the flame kindle upon thee.

Going through rivers of difficulty will either cause you to frown or force you to grow stronger. God said in do not remember the former things all these things happen in the pass. When you go through struggles do you doubt God's goodness or that he cares about you. Jesus has made it plain the cost of discipleship, if anyone would come after me let him deny himself and take up his cross daily and follow me. Paul followed the Lord's example of commitment, Paul said I have been crucified with Christ It is no longer I who live but Christ who lives in me. The life I now live in the flesh I live by Faith in the son of God who loved me and gave Himself for me.

When you go out, witness to somebody tell them about the glory in your story. Some people look at you and think that you never had no downs. They think you have always been up; I have had some ups and downs. Tell them that there is Glory in your story. Tell them that you have had some hardships some time you had to cry. Jesus never promised that obeying him would be easy work.

To develop a lifestyle of prayer in our lives, we need to have that same calmness of spirit. To achieve that, we must first prepare our hearts and minds for prayer. We wouldn't think of going on a long car trip without checking the map to see where we're going, packing what we'll need, and making sure our car is in working condition and has a full tank of gas. In the same way, we need to prepare ourselves for prayer. Our road map is God's Word, we should study it to know God's promises and direction for our life. We should have no excess baggage on our trip, which means we need to clear away any distractions so we can focus fully on aligning ourselves with our Redeemer in prayer. In addition, to make sure we are in working condition, we need to clean our thoughts, have the right attitude for prayer and have the right relationship with God and others. In addition, God commands us, along with Joshua to learn His Word and speak it in prayer to receive his blessings by learning His Word.

Be still before the Lord and wait patiently for him (Psalm 37:7) When we are in prayer with God, we need to be focused solely on Him-to "be still" as the psalmist says, seeking to hear His voice in our life. In prayer, as in everything our motives are very important. If we ask for things to please ourselves or impress others, we have the wrong motives. If we are after what we can get for ourselves rather than being surrendered to God and his will, our prayers are not proper. (James 4:3) "When you ask, you do not receive because you ask with wrong motives that you may spend what you get on your pleasures."

Often we really want God to be something he is not. There is a god we want and a God who is, and they are not the same. Many times, we do not understand God. (Isaiah 55:8) "For my thoughts are not your thoughts, neither are your ways my ways, declares the Lord." It is through prayer that we begin to get a glimpse of who God really is. We begin to learn who he wants us to be. Therefore, in our prayer lives we need a proper gaze, focused on Jesus Christ. If we allow gaze to be on our requests, those requests will consume us. We end up telling God what we need to be done; we attempt control him.

As we said earlier one of the reasons we pray is to receive from God. He wants to provide for us, he also wants our thoughts and motives in line with his will. So we pray to God almighty as our Redeemer and Savior, seeking his will in our lives and having faith that he will provide for our every need. (Psalm 37:4) assures us of this: "Delight yourself in the Lord and he will give you the desires of your heart."

If our prayers were answered for the wrong reasons, we would continue to come to God for what we get from him. We would continue to pray so we could gain material goods. Our selfishness would be fed, and we would not recognize that we should surrender our will to God.

When we ask of God, we should ask in His name for His will to be done. Jesus tells us in (John 16:23-24) "I tell you the truth, my Father will give you whatever you ask in his name. Until now, you have not asked for anything in my name. Ask and you will receive it and your joy will be complete." When we do that, we hand Him our selfishness, our desire for control, our desire for worldly possessions. We have a feeling of love that is a result of God redeeming us from our sin. Does prayer change events? It may, nevertheless the most important effect of prayer is that it changes the person who is praying to become more like the one to whom he is praying—our Redeemer.

In the same way that we clean our thoughts and make sure we have the right motives in prayer, we also must clean our hearts of sin against our Lord. If we try to pray, but at the same time trying to hide sin from him, we create a wall that prayer cannot overcome. We must be prepared to be honest with God, to confess our sins and our weakness. He knows them already, nevertheless in being honest with our Lord, we seek reunion with Him and can be made whole with Him again. (Psalm 66:18-19) says, "If I had cherished sin in my heart the Lord would not have listened, but God has surely listened and heard my voice in prayer."

Anyone who claims to be in the light, but hates his brother is still in the darkness. (1 John 2:9). In the same way that we reconcile our relationship with God, we must reconcile our relationships with others. In addition just as God forgives our sins, so we must forgive others (Mark 11:25) says "and when you stand praying, if you hold anything against anyone, forgive him, so that your Father in heaven may forgive you your sins."

The greatest part of prayer is to forgive others. Righteousness, which is the ultimate aspect of the Christian walk, is impossible to achieve until we have been forgiven and in turn forgive. Unless we forgive, we can never be in a true relationship with the Lord and be able to do the things he would have us to do. To prepare ourselves for prayer we must be ready to listen to our Redeemer. It takes time, effort and practice to put the distractions of the world work, we also must always put ourselves on the line to have an open honest and joyous relationship with God in prayer.

We have to be vigilant in making sure our motives are aligned with God's motives. In addition, we must be honest with him about the sins that keep us from being inclined to him. In the same way we must have open relationship with others. It can be hard work but the benefits far out weight the risks. Therefore, we do not lose heart however outwardly we are wasting away yet inwardly we are renewed day by day. For our light and momentary troubles are achieving for us and eternal glory that far outweighs them all.

Therefore, we fix our eyes not on what is seen, but on what is unseen. For what is seen is temporary, but what is unseen is eternal. (II Corinthians 4:16-18) The person that has found Jesus and who has Jesus Christ dwelling within them, is listening to Our Lord talk constantly to their, conscience, soul, and spirit. The true child of God can hear God speaks to their mind. God speaks to their sense of moral righteousness and fairness. To their sense of what is right and Godly. In addition, those methods of communication that God uses are extremely loud and clear.

The person that has found Jesus and who has Jesus Christ dwelling within them, is listening to Our Lord talk constantly to their heart, conscience, soul and spirit. The true child of God can hear God speak just as clearly, as if God was standing right along, side of them verbally talking to them. However before God can begin to talk to you, something must happen. You have to be receptive to God's words. You have to begin to communicate with God and listen for God to speak. You have to get your heart in the right condition.

"Prayer is the answer to every problem in life. It puts us in tune with divine wisdom, which knows how to adjust everything perfectly. So

often, do not pray in certain situations, because from our standpoint the outlook is hopeless. But remember no mind is so dull that it cannot be made brilliant. Whatever we need, if we trust God, he will supply it. If anything is causing worry or anxiety, let us stop rehearsing the difficulty and trust God for healing, love and power."

Every believer is involved in spiritual warfare, the problems we face are brought about by satanic principalities, powers, rulers of darkness of this world and wicked spirits in heavenly places. Our responsibility is to use the weapons of our warfare to fight the good fight of faith, what are those weapons? The name of Jesus the Word of God, the Holy Spirit and the gifts of the Spirit are major defense weapons on the battlefield of prayer.

Prayer is the battlefield. The time spent in prayer is the base of supply. The armor described in (Ephesians 6) is prayer armor. It serves one vital purpose: to combat Satan and win! Your enemy is other people. Satan is the source of all your trouble. Some people believe that God sends tribulation and trials. However, God has provided the weapons and armor that get us out of trouble, Satan is the trouble maker God is not the trouble, our neighbor is not the trouble, our co-worker is not the problem.

As long as you see yourself unworthy, you will not experience answered prayer to any heart degree. An understanding of righteousness will put you on the road to success. You have the right to resist Satan and to expect him to flee. The Word says "Above all, taking the shield of faith," Your shield quenches all of the fiery darts of the wicked. (1 John 5:4) says, "And this is the victory that over cometh the world even our faith." Your faith makes you an over comer and more than a conqueror! "The just shall live by faith" (Romans 1:17). This mean your whole life is sustained by your faith in God. Finally, "Take the helmet of salvation." A helmet is protection for the head. (Romans 12:2) says, "And be not conformed to this world: but be ye transformed by the renewing of your mind, that ye may prove what is that good, and acceptable, and perfect, will of God. Satan's battleground is your mind. By keeping your mind renewed to the Word of God.

(Philippians 2:9-10), "God also hath highly exalted him, and give a name which is above every name: That at the name of Jesus every knee should bow, of things in heaven, and things in earth, and things under the earth." In Jesus name, the believer has authority to tread on serpents and scorpions and over all the power of the enemy "(Luke 10:19). Satan knows the power vested in that name and he will retreat when it is spoken in faith (James 4:7)." One translation says to stand up to the Devil and he will turn and run.

Prayer is an attitude it involves more than just making requests. Prayer is communicating with God, you can live in an attitude of prayer constantly, being in communion and fellowship with your heavenly father every hour of the day.

In order to get results in prayer, you must be convinced of one basic fact: God wants to answer your prayers, in fact he is as ready and willing to answer you, as he was to answer Jesus during his early ministry. This may be difficult for you to believe, but it is true.

When you pray the prayer of salvation, you may not feel differently, realize that your feeling do not have anything to do with it. **God's word is His part of your prayer life,** He has already said in His Word, "Thou shalt be saved." You allowed the Word of God to engineer your prayer it makes no difference how you feel, Exercise your faith. The authority of God's Word saves you. In (Mark 11:24) Jesus said what things so ever ye desire, when ye pray, believe that ye receive them, and ye shall have them. The kind of prayer that moves mountains is prayer for the fruitfulness of God's Kingdom. It would seem impossible to move a mountain into the sea, so Jesus used that picture to show that God can do anything.

God will answer your prayers, but not as a result of your positive mental attitude. Other conditions must be met (1) You must believe; (2) you must not hold a grudge against another person; (3) you must not pray with selfish motives; (4) your request must be for the good of the kingdom, to pray effectively, you need faith in God, not faith in the object of your request. If you focus only on your request, you will be left with nothing if your request is refused.

Jesus, our example, once prayed, "All things are possible unto thee; nevertheless not what I will, but what thou wilt" Our prayers are often motivated by our own interests and desires. We like to hear that we can have anything. But Jesus prayed with God's interests in mind. When we pray, we can express our desires, but we should want his will above ours. Check yourself to see if your prayers focus on your interests or God's.

Praying for healing involves the same faith principles. Search God's Word for your answer, (Isaiah 53:5), "But he was wounded for our transgressions, he was bruised for our iniquities: the chastisement of our peace was upon him; and with his stripes we are healed." (Matthew 8:17) says "himself took our infirmities and bear our sicknesses." Undoubtedly healing is God's will, according to these words, Jesus paid the price –not only for sin, but also for sickness, disease and the consequences of sin. Traditions that are more religious have discounted God's will for healing than those that discredit salvation. To know God's will towards healing, look at Jesus who said, he that seen me hath seen the" Father (John 14:9). During his time on earth, Jesus was the express image of God (Hebrews 1:3). What did he do? He healed the sick, (Acts 10:38) says, God anointed Jesus of Nazareth with the Holy Ghost and power: who went about doing good, and healing all that were oppressed of the devil; for God was with him."

The prayer for healing is a simple one. You say, Father in the name of Jesus, I see in your word that healing belongs to me. I believe I receive it I thank you for it, I act upon it now." Once you have prayed,

TRUST. Do not let Satan convince you that you are still sick. He will try his best to sell his lies. **Stand your ground!** Say" Satan it is written…" Then begin to speak what God's word says about your healing just as he fled at the command of Jesus' words. Satan will have to flee when you speak God's word in faith (Matthew 4:1-11). He has no defense against the word of God when a believer speaks it in faith. A very misunderstood concept throughout the religious world is that it is extremely difficult to get God to answer prayer at all-much less answer all prayer. That is a lie of Satan and absolutely contrary to the Word of God. **When you believe God's Word in your heart and you pray in line with His Word, you have every right to expect your prayer to bring results.** Jesus said: "Verily I say unto you, if ye have faith, and doubt not, ye shall not only do this which is done to the fig tree, but also if ye shall say unto this mountain, be thou removed. And be thou cast into the sea; it shall be done. And all thing, whatsoever ye shall ask in prayer, believing, ye shall receive (Matthew 21:21-22). If God will answer the prayer of a sinner to be saved, He will certainly answer the prayers of born-again believers who come to Him in faith concerning their lives. Satan uses doubt and fear to bluff you into accepting defeat,

You can overcome him by the power of God and faith in his Word. You can avoid failure by preparing to succeed. Once you have prayed in faith, you must stand your ground until them manifestation come. Fight the good fight of faith. Stand firm on the Word and believe God for results. Give him the opportunity to do something with your circumstances. God is on your side! Prepare to succeed, not to fail. When you pray in Jesus' Name, according to the Word in Faith, God Will quickly respond to you (John16:23). Suppose you prayed for healing, then you think what will I do if God does not heal me? Maybe I had better get an appointment with the doctor. He is very busy this time of the year. you might not be able to see him, then if God does not heal you, you will be hurt! With that attitude believing God will be a waste of time. The person who thinks that way will be unable to receive from God. Before he prays, he is already preparing to fail. He is double minded and, according to (James 1:8), unstable in all his ways. The man who wavers in his mind will never receive from God. He is like a wave of the sea, driven with the wind and tossed about in every direction. He has a backup plan "just in case." The moment he feels the least bit sick, he will operate in fear and unbelief. When he feels well, he will act in faith, but he will never achieve any concrete results.

(John14:14) If ye shall ask anything in my name, I will do it. When Jesus says we can ask for anything, we must remember that our asking must be in his name—that is, according to God's character and will. God will not grant requests contrary to his nature or his will, and we cannot use his name as a magic formula to fulfill our selfish desires. If we are sincerely following God and seeking to do his will, then our requests will be in line with what he wants, and he will grant them.

(Hebrews 5:16) Let us therefore come boldly unto the throne of grace, that we may obtain mercy, and find grace to help in time of need. Prayer is our approach to God, and we are to come "boldly unto the throne of grace." Some Christians approach God meekly with heads hung, afraid to ask to meet their needs. Others pray flippantly with little thought. Come with reverence, for he is your King. But also come with bold assurance, for he is your Friend and Counselor.

You don't have to isolate yourself from other people and from daily work in order to pray constantly. You can make prayer your life, we are living in a world that needs God's powerful influence.

When you believe God's word in your heart and you pray in line with his word, you have every right to expect your prayer to bring results. (Matthew 21:21-22)If ye have faith, and doubt not, ye shall not only do this which is done to the fig tree, but also if ye shall say unto this mountain. Be thou removed and be thou cast into the sea; it shall be done. And all things whatsoever ye shall ask in prayer, believing ye shall receive. If God will answer the prayer of a sinner to be saved, he will certainly answer the prayers of born-again believers who come to him in faith concerning their lives.

Ask God to help you with your prayer, God is not only able to answer your prayer, but he is also able to make your prayer, but he is also able to make your prayer to him stronger. The power of your prayers will increase dramatically when you realize that God has all power. "I of mine own self can do nothing, It is the Father in me which doeth the work." In prayer, it is the Divine within you appealing to the divine above.

The Divine within you is a part of God that he has placed within you as his child. In an ordinary conversation, we speak and then listen for the response of the other person it is the same with God! Once we have prepared our hearts to listen through prayer, we are more likely to hear the voice of God. Does he speak to us through an audible voice? Some claim he does, but usually that is not the case. We may not actually "hear" the voice of God, but he speaks to us in many ways. Here are some of them:

God speaks through His Word

God speaks through our thoughts

God speaks through conversations with others

God speaks through circumstances

Everything we need we can find it in Jesus. Obtaining the things we need or want we ask God. Through prayer, we talk to God about all our cares, "Cast thy burden upon the Lord, and he shall sustain: he shall never suffer the righteous to be moved."

(Matthew 6:7) "But when ye pray, use not vain repetitions, as the heathen do, for they think that they shall be heard for their much speaking." The beauty of your prayer does not get the ear of God. He responds to faith. To explain let me give you an example from my own experience, not long after I became a Christian, I asked a pastor to pray for me. I was expecting to hear a long beautiful prayer, one that would cause people to fall on their knees in repentance before God. What I heard was just the opposite. He laid his hand on my head, bowed his head and said, "Lord bless her, meet her every need." He then turned and walked away. I was left standing there thinking how could he do this to me?

It makes no difference how long you pray, or how beautiful your words. **Praying in faith is merely having confidence in God's willingness to use His power to answer your prayer.** The man or woman who knows the importance of prayer is very difficult to defeat, regardless of what comes, he can pray and God will move in his behalf.

The key to success in prayer is expecting results, many Christians think, I will pray and maybe something will happen. They say, "I'm just hoping and praying." If you are hoping to get results, you will never receive from God. "Hoping to get" is not the same as "believing you receive." The promises of God bring you hope in hopeless situations however, hope has no substance in itself. "I hope to receive somedays, but someday never come. **Faith brings hope into reality and give substance to it. (Hebrews 11:1) says, "Now faith is the substance of things hoped for, the evidence of things not seen."**

The object of hope becomes a reality through faith hope is always in the future faith is always now. The number one rule in praying for results are based on your prayer on God's Word. It can be relied on just as you would depend on the word of your best friend. If you trust him, you will believe what he says. Faith in God operates the same way God's word is the integrity of God Himself. Some of you pray and pray, but your prayers are not heard. You had as well never offer them any more until you make a genuine effort to pay the bills you owe, to right the wrongs you have done, to apologize for sins committed and to be reconciled with others. Oh what zeal we ought to have about making wrongs right! Jesus said, "Ye have heard that it hath been said, an eye for an eye, and a tooth for a tooth: but I say unto you, that ye resist not evil: but whosoever shall smite thee on thy right cheek turn to him the other also.

What is righteousness? It is having right actions, right attitudes, and right relationships, all based on our right standing with God. When he forgives us, takes away our sin, and restores us as his children, he not only gives us his righteousness, but he also empowers us to demonstrate it to others.

The power of pray is the sincerity in the heart. Religious prayers do not come from the heart. Great results come from earnest not loudness. Supplication is the most common form of prayer where in a person asks a supernatural deity (God) to provide something, either for that person who is praying or for someone else on whose behalf a prayer of supplication. A successful prayer is based on the written word of God. If you do not know the word of God, you are begging God not praying an effective prayer.

Why does it seem that some Christians get their prayers answered and others do not?

CHAPTER

THE POWER OF PRAYER

Let us look at the word supplication, we come to God in prayer for man and woman we come to God in Prayer for many reasons. To worship him and to confess our sins, for ourselves and to pray, to worship him to confess our sins and ask for forgiveness and to thank Him for His blessings. To ask for things for ourselves and to pray, for the needs of others, so a prayer of supplication is asking God for something. (Psalm 5:8) David was asking for deliverance.

(Luke18:1-8) Jesus teaches us not to give up praying for what we need, not what we want but need. Supplications is to ask and don't receive as children talking to their kindhearted Father. But ending with your will be done. In full surrender to His will, Prayers of supplication are part of the spiritual battle all Christians are engaged in it.

Prayers of supplication is there is no faith, these is no need of praying we have got to have faith that our prayers will be answer. When we began to pray to Jesus the indwelling Holy Spirit interpreter on our behalf, because we often don't know what or how to pray when we approach God. The spirit intercedes and prays for us its interpreter our supplication so when we are overwhelmed by trials and the cares of life. He assistance us without prayers I am just like Paul as a believer we are not left by ourselves with our problem.

Have you ever been to the point you don't know the right worlds to pray? You open your mouth and nothing come out, at this time the Holy Spirit Prays with and for you. There was a Lady telling me, Dr. Hall I was so hurt I just went down on my knees and cried. I just could not get a word out.

If you want to know who Jesus really is try the impossible, let me tell you when you try the impossible you will find out that he will make a way out of no way. When your back is up against the wall and it does not look like there is no way out Jesus will put a door where there is no door. Jesus specializes in things that seem to be impossible to stringing our faith believe and trust him. All we have to do is stand back just say Lord work it out. If you want to know who Jesus really is? Try the impossible, let me tell you when you try the impossible you will find out that he will make a way out of no way. When your back is up against the wall and it does not look like there is no way out, Jesus will put a door where there is no door. Jesus specialize in things that seem to be impossible to stringing out faith believe and trust him. You remember in the book of (Acts 12) Peter was put in prison and the word reached the Christian, and they all call pray meeting at sister Mary house. As this little band prayed God didn't answer their prayers immediately. They didn't stop praying they called on the one who had all power we call Him Jesus never give up on Jesus.

Peter laid there between sixteen soldiers he was not worry he had turn everything over to Jesus. At midnight pray meeting was still going on at Sister Mary house. When we pray and pray, seem like nothing is going to happen, Jesus does not hear my pray, that when the impossible happen. An angle of the Lord enter the prison. He stood by Peter, Peter arise quickly the chains fell off his hands and feet.

He said Gird yourself put on your sandals put on your coat and follow me Peter was dealing with the impossible He thought that He was seeing a vison. They walk through the 1st gate the gauds didn't see them they walk through the 2nd gate. Then walk through the big iron gate. Look at God working He work the impossible for you. When I think of all his goodness and all he has done for me I have to give Him glory, I got to give Him glory, I got to praise Him. If God didn't give us no rough roads to walk- is he didn't, if he didn't give us no mountains to climb.

If he didn't give us no battles to fight we wouldn't grow. Some time it takes trials and tribulations to keep you and I humble. Sometime it takes trials to keep us on our knees.

God's word is his will, when you pray in line with the word, you have automatically prayed in line with God's will. 1 John 5:14:15, And this is the confidence that we have in him that if we ask any thing according to his will, he heareth us: God's word operates in the spiritual realm. Our responsibility is to use the spiritual weapons at our disposal, for though we walk in the flesh, we do not war after the flesh. For the weapons of our warfare are not carnal, but mighty through God to the pulling down of strong holds. Maintain control of your mind do not allow doubt or fear to enter your consciousness. Be ready to refuse any thought or imagination contrary to your prayer. When doubt comes refuse to give it any place be selective about the thoughts you entertain. Control your thought life according to Philippians 4:6-9. Learn to think on things that are true, honest, just, pure, lovely, and of good report.

Understanding prayer is stating what it is not. Pray is not an emotional release, prayer is not a means of escape. Prayer is more than asking God for a favor. Prayer is not a religious exercise, praying should be for getting results every time you pray. Do not just speak empty words. Matthew 6:8 "But when ye pray, use not vain repetitions, as the heathen do: for they think that they shall be heard for their much speaking." Be not ye therefore like unto them: for your Father knows what things ye have need of, before ye ask him.

Repeating the same words over and over like a magic incantation is no way to ensure that God will hear your prayer. It's not wrong to come to God many times with the same requests – Jesus encourages persistent prayer. But he condemns the shallow repetition of words that are not offered with a sincere heart. We can never pray too much if our prayers are honest and sincere.

Jesus provided a pattern to be imitated as well as duplicated. We should praise God, pray for his work in the world, pray for our daily needs, and pray for help in our daily struggles. To what extent do you use the items in the Lord's prayer to guide, God's word is His will. When you pray in line with the Word, you have automatically prayed in line with God's will. 1 John 5:14-15) says, and this is the confidence that we have in him, that if we ask any thing according to his will, he heareth us. And if we know that he here us whatsoever we ask, we know that we have the petitions that we desired of him. Your prayer for salvation, based on God is word was clearly heard by the Father. After you pray and receive your salvation by faith, you then simply thank God for it.

(2 Corinthians 5:17) says, If any man be in Christ he is a new creature: old things are passed away; behold all things are become new. See yourself as a new creation. The man you once were died the death of the cross and was raised to new life by the power of the Holy Spirit. This is actually what happened. You prayed according to the Word of God, therefore you are saved. Praying for healing involves the same faith principles.

The prayer for healing is a simple one, you say "Father in the Name of Jesus, I see in your Word that healing belongs to me. I believe I receive it. I thank you for it, I act upon it now." Once you have prayer, do not let Satan convince you that you are still sick. He will try his best to sell his lies. Stand your ground! "Satan, it is written" Then begin to speak what God's Word says about your healing. Just as he fled at the command of Jesus' words, Satan will have to flee when you speak

God's Word in faith (Matthew 4:1-11). He has no defense against the Work of God when a believer speaks it in faith.

When you begin your prayer based on God's Word, you are starting with the answer. The Word contains the answer to every problem that could confront you.

(Mark 11:24) Therefore I say unto you, what things so ever ye desire, when ye pray, believe that ye receive them, and ye shall have them. Jesus, our example, once prayed, "All things are possible unto thee; nevertheless not what I will, but what thou wilt." Our prayers are often motivated by our interests and desires. We like to hear that we can have anything. Jesus prayed with God's interests in mind. When we pray, we can express our desires, but we should want his will above ours. Check yourself to see if your prayers focus on your interests or God's.

When you pray, all you have to do is apply your faith. Where does faith come from? How do you get faith? (Romans 10:17) Faith come by hearing and hearing by the Word of God. (Romans 12:3) Every believe is dealt the measure of faith. He must develop that faith by spending time in the Word of God. The application of your faith in any given situation is directly related your knowledge of God. If you feel that you need more faith, realize that you already have faith. What you need is a more personal knowledge of God through time in the Word.

Once you have prayed in faith, hold fast to your confession, God is aware of your situation. His power went to work the instant you prayed in faith. You can rest assured that what you prayed will happen. Maintain your faith by keeping your confession in line with the Word. The word of God is quick, powerful, and sharper than any two-edged sword, piercing even to the dividing asunder of soul and spirit, and of the joints and marrow, and is a discerner of the thoughts and intents of the heart. Neither is there any creature that is not manifest in his sight: but all things are naked and opened unto the eyes of him with whom have to do. Seeing then that we have a great high priest that is passed into the heavens, Jesus the Son of God let us hold fast our profession.

Once you have prayed, hold fast to your confession. Refuse to speak contrary to the word of God. Do not allow circumstances to sway you. Act as though it were already done. When you apply your faith accurately according to God's Word, you will get results. You will experience (Hebrews 4:16) for yourself, Let us therefore come boldly unto the throne of grace, that we may obtain mercy, and find grace to help in time of need. It does not say, "Come and hope to get." It says, "Come obtain mercy and find grace to help in time of need.

Prayer is our approach to God, and we are to come "boldly unto the throne of grace." Some Christians approach God meekly with heads hanging, afraid to ask him to meet their needs. Others pray flippantly with little thought. Come with reverence, for he is your King. But also come with bold assurance, for he is your Friend and Counselor.

(Isaiah 40:31) they that wait upon the Lord shall renew their strength they shall mount up with wings as eagles. They shall run and not be weary they shall walk and not faint. Isaiah is saying be patient, trust God to do what he promises. God is not slack concerning His promises. We are blessed for success, God has healing with your on it. New dream with your name on it promotions with your name on it because he fine favor in you.

Some of your long prays God never hears them, and some of you give much money; and the sight of it is an abomination to God. Some of you work and toil doing "church work," and God hate it. Anything you can offer to God is hateful in his sight if you will not go and be reconciled to others you have wronged. There is a fundamental hypocrisy in any attempt at worship or service by those who do not honestly forsake sin and make an effort to undo the wrong that has been done, to pay debts that have been made, to ask forgiveness for sins committed against other.

Many of people cannot get their prayers heard because already God has heard the cry of others whom they have wronged. Cain tried to talk to God; but the blood of his slain brother Abel, had cried out of the ground to God against Cain. Some people pray and pray, but your prayers are not heard you had as well never offer them any more until you make a genuine effort to pay the bills you owe, to right the wrongs you have done, to apologize for sins committed and to be reconciled with other. It praying time, it is time to stop doing our brothers and sisters wrong.

(John 15:12) This is my commandment, that ye love one another, as I have you. I have a question? While people can't love one another and most of them go to church, and love the Jesus they say. We have got to love one another; a person is a slave to whatever controls him. Many believe freedom means doing anything you want. But no one is ever completely free in that sense. If we refuse to follow God, we will follow our own sinful desires and become enslaved to what our bodies want. If we submit our lives to Christ, he will free us from slavery of sin. Christ frees us to serve him, resulting in our ultimate good.

CHAPTER 7

FAITH IN THE MIDDLE OF A STROM

Make a Joyful Noise unto the LORD all ye land serve the LORD with gladness come before his presence with singing. Know ye that the Lord he is God it is he that hath made us and not we ourselves, we are his people and the sheep of his pasture.

Enter into his gates with thanksgiving and into his courts with praise be thankful unto him and bless his name. God brought us, He kept his arms around us, oh yes we had some trails and tribulation sometime we had to cry, but he brought us.

He wakes us up every morning, if you are reading this book right now; you need to stop: and tell the LORD THANK YOU.

We see Wars, Nation Against Nation, Famines, Earthquakes, Jesus say in (Matthew Ch24) All these are the beginning of sorrows, killing, and shall betray one another, The Love of many will wax cold. So many places we go people will ask what do you think about CORONAVIRUS that killing thousands of people all over the world. I think it is God work, if you are lost don't know Jesus Christ you are lost, he want you to turn around from your sinful ways and be saved. come to him while you have a change, this simply mean that God's program is running on time. It nothing to soon and nothing too late.

God promises great blessings to his people but many of these blessing require active participation.

(James 4:8) tell us to draw nigh to God and he will draw nigh to you, James is telling us that we have to have FAITH in the middle of the storm. How can we draw close to God? (1) Submit to God we have got to realize that we need his forgiveness and be willing to follow him. (2) Resist the Devil don't allow him to leave you into his tempt. James is telling us to be clean from sin (3) Humble yourself before God, and he will lift you up.

We wish we could escape troubles, the pains, of grief, the loss, the sorrow, and the failure, even the small daily frustrations that constantly wear us down, but we can't we have got to go through. God promises to carry us through, He promise to be with us and never leave us. It is good that we don't know when he is coming If we knew exactly when Christ will return. If we knew the precise date, we might be tempted to be lazy in our work for Christ. We might keep sinning and then turn to God right at the end, The Gospel is not only what we believe but also what we must live. The Holy Spirit leads us in faithfulness, so we can avoid lust and fraud. Live as though you expect Christ's return at any time. Don't be caught unprepared

When we dwell on your problems, we will become anxious and angry, But God want us to concentrate on his goodness. Out of all David went through, He kept a humble attitude, when you dwell on your problems you will become anxious and angry. David said I will bless the Lord at all times, David knew real help comes from God alone when a situation seen out of control.

God sent his angels to protect you and I from physical and spiritual harm. There is a song that say-all night and all day the angels keep over watching over me. Let us all ways remember God loves us and he is in control. We should not fret and worry, instead we should trust in the LORD, give yourself to God for his use and safekeeping we can't keep our self. When we dwell on our problems we will become anxious and angry. But God want us to concentrate on his goodness, Out of all David went through he kept a humble attitudes, when you dwell on your problems you will become anxious, angry David say I will bless the Lord at all times.

God is so good, somebody might want to know how do you know, do you know him as your LORD and Savior, remember He wake you up early this morning, He didn't let you sleep too late. You have your health. Then you went down to your breakfast table and told the LORD, I am thankful I am so thankful that early this morning you didn't, let us sleep too late. We got up right on time He put food on our table, cloths on our back, if it had not been for the LORD on our side, where would we be, what would we do? He is a good GOD. When I was on my sick bed He was right there.

How do you know God is good? Just tell them that God lives down in your heart. I know he is good. When we call upon God. He will answered sometime in an unexpected way, God knows our every need, and our deepest needs are spiritual. All of our needs are God, and many hardships come with having God but God is still enough. Because He is out Creator, He is Lord, Our Savior, and He is our Deliver, He is our Dr. on our sick bed, He is our bread in a stocking land,

I will strengthen you I will help you I will uphold you with my righteous right hand. In the storm of life, we away say I got It, it's under control. There will be storms in our life's some time Jesus will move them, and some time He will get on board and ride them out with us.

God is speaking all over the world, telling men and women to turn from sin. He is telling people to come unto me all ye that labor, and are heavy laden and I will give you rest. Take my yoke upon you and learn of me I am meek and in heart and you shall find rest unto your souls. Jesus tells us that his yoke is easy and my burden is light. Jesus frees people from all these burdens and the rest he promises is love, healing, and peace with God.

Jesus specialized in things that seem to be impossible to stringing our faith believe and trust him. All we have to do is stand back and just say Lord works it out. Peter was put in Prison and the word reached the Christians, and they call a pray meeting at sister Mary house. This little band prayed, God did not answer their prayers immediately. They didn't stop praying they called on the one who had all power. They call on Jesus, never give up on JESUS.

Peter laid there he was sleeping because he had turned ever thing over to Jesus. At midnight pray meeting was still going on at sister Mary House. When we pray and pray that is when the impossible happen. Angle of the Lord enter the prison. He not only enter the prison, he stood by peter he touch him and said arise quickly and the chains fell off his hands and feet. Gird yourself put on your sandals, put on your coat and follow me. Peter was dealing with the impossibilities It's Praying Time.

In Acts Ch 27, We read where Paul was on a ship with 276 others in the middle of a violent storm. At one point Paul step forward to tell them all to be of good cheer. God encourage those who suffer for him to just trust him, we are not rejoicing because we are going through a storm. We are rejoicing only because we know that God some way, somehow will see us through. We have got to trust him and keep the FAITH and be patience. The storms of life come when we are not looking, it's not a cloud day the sun is bright and pretty. It's not even raining setting back thinking everything is fine. And all of such outcome a storm, we don't know how to deal with a storm. One good thing about a storm they are temporary they don't last always.

A spiritual Storm is an unpredictable temporary period of distress over which we have little if any control. Paul referred to the storm in his life as a light affliction, which last but for a moment. (Psalm 108:13) Through God we shall do valiantly: for he it is that shall tread down our enemies. Do your prayers end with requests for help to make it through stressful situations? David prayed not merely for rescue but for victory! Look for ways God can use your distress as an opportunity to show his might power.

You should be praying for results every time you pray. Do not just speak empty words, Jesus said in (Matthew 6:7) "But when ye pray, use not vain repetition, as the heathen do for they think that they shall be heard for their much speaking." The beauty of your prayer does not get the ear of God. He responds to faith. To explain, let me give you an example from my own experience, not long after I became a Christian, I asked a minister to pray for me. I was expecting to hear a long beautiful prayer - - one that would cause people to fall on their knees in repentance before God! What I heard was just the opposite. He laid his hand on my chest, bowed his head, and said "LORD, bless her. Meet her every need," he then turned and walked away.

Praying in faith is merely having confidence in God's willingness to use His power to answer your prayer. The man who knows the importance of prayer is very difficult to defeat. He knows that regardless of what comes he can pray and God will move in his behalf. The key to success in prayer is expecting results. Many Christians think I will pray and may be something will happen, they say I am just hoping and praying. If you are hoping to get results, you will never receive from God. "Hoping to get" is not the same as "believing you receive." The promises of God bring you hope in hopeless situations, however hope has no substance in itself. "I hope to get healed someday." You hope to receive someday, but someday never come.

Every believer is involved in spiritual warfare, the problems we face are brought about by satanic forces. Principalities, powers, rulers, of darkness of this world and wicked spirits in heavenly places. Our responsibility is to use the weapons of our warfare to fight the good fight of faith. What are those weapons? The Name of Jesus, the Word of God, the Holy Spirit and the gifts of the Spirit are major defense weapons on the battlefield of prayer. The time in prayer is the base of supply, the armor described in (Ephesians 6) is prayer armor to serves one vital purpose: It service one.

God is all seeing, all-showing, all-knowing, all-holy, all- present, God is with us, and his greatest gift is to allow us to know him.

Pray for protection against those who slander, or threaten. Deliverance become as we focus on our future life with God. You should be praying for results every time you pray. Do not just speak empty words. Jesus said in (Matthew 5:7) "But when ye pray, use not vain repetitions, as the heathen do: for as the beauty of your prayer does not get the ear of God. He responds to faith. Praying in faith is merely having confidence in God's willingness to use His power to answer your prayer.

Faith does not make anything thing easy, but it does make all thing possible. You are covered armor of God. The armor of God is strong and stands against any attack of the enemy. Let me show you how it works "And having done all, to stand. Stand therefore, having your lions girt about with truth. When Satan tells you that you will never see the manifestation of your prayers is the time to gird yourself with the. God's Word is everything. God alone has the right to be jealous and to carry our vengeance with God Jealousy and vengeance may be surprising terms to associate with God. He is slow to get angry, but when he is ready to punish, even the earth trembles. Often people avoid God because they see evildoers in the world and hypocrites in the church. They don't realize that because God is slow to anger, he gives his true followers time to share his love and truth with evildoers. But judgment will come; God will not allow sin to go unchecked forever. When people wonder why God doesn't punish evil immediately, help them remember that if he did, none of us would be here. We can all be thankful that God gives people time to turn to him.

Jesus said in Matthew 6:22, "The light of the body is the eye; if therefore thine eye be single, thy whole body shall be full of light.' Your body responds to what it is fed through eyes. If you are believing God for healing you must feed your consciousness with the Word of God which will bring healing. Waste no time on useless activities. Be diligent to diligent to spend your time in God's word. The Word of God will set you free. Make plains to succeed It's Praying Time, what is pray? Pray is a conversation of the heart with God. Have you had your conversation with God today?

Evening, morning and at noon will I pray and cry aloud, He shall hear my voice. David said my heart is sore pained within me and terrors of death are fallen upon me. Fearfulness and trembling are come upon me and horror hath overwhelmed me. And I said oh that I had wings like a dove for then would I fly away and be at rest.

David is telling us I'm close to God I am a man after his heart. but I have moments when I want to get away from it all, and escape problems and pressures. It is when you are doing the best you can and people just don't understand when you know it by God word the Devil don't want to understand. He wants to keep something going all the time.

(PS 55:12) David said for it was not an enemy that reproached me, then I could have bear it. Neither was it he that hated me that did magnify himself against me, then I would have hide myself from him. David was saying, nothing hurts as much as a wound from a friend. He was in trouble. He needed his friends but he was Betrayal by a friend caused David great anguish, real friends stick by you in time of trouble help you heal. David was hurting when friends hurt us the burden is too difficult to carry along.

PRAY AND TIME

Pray when we are surrounded by trouble or God is our only real source of safety. Prayer is our best help when trials come our way, because it keeps us in communion with God. God is creator he is Lord our savior and is creator, he is Lord, our savor, and deliver. God sent His angels to protect you and I from physical and spiritual harm. There is a song that say It all day, and it's all night Jesus kept watching over me let us all ways remember God loves us.(Ephesians 6:18) Praying always with all prayer and supplication in the Spirit, and watching there unto with all perseverance and supplication for all saints;

How can anyone pray all the time? One way to pray constantly is to make quick, brief prayers your habitual response to is to order your life around God's desires and teachings so that your very life become a prayer. You don't have to isolate yourself from other people and from daily work in order to pray constantly. You can make prayer your life and your life a prayer while living in a world that needs God's powerful influence.

The godly are those who are faithful and devoted to God. David knew that God would hear him when he called and would answer him, too, can be confident that God listens and answers when we call on him. Sometimes we think God will not hear us because we have fallen short of his high standards for holy living. But God has forgiven us and he will listen to us. When you feel that your prayers are "bouncing off the ceiling," remember that as a believer you have been set apart by God and that he loves you. He hears and answers (although his answers may not be what you expect). Look at your problems in the light of God's power instead of looking at God in the shadow of your problems.

The only way to obtain the promises of God is praying in faith. Faith is a spiritual principle that taps into the supernatural power of God that is made available to man whereby man can transform his circumstance, situations, and conditions in the natural realm over which he has been given authority. The first step in praying a pray of faith is qualify your desire. Make sure that what you want to release faith for lines up with the word of God. Second, ask God for what you desire according to the word of God. Third, believe. After you ask God for what you desire, it is imperative for you to believe at that very moment, It's Done! Fourth, confess. Confess the word of God over your situation no matter what it looks like around you.

CHAPTER 8

THE VALLEY IS TEMPORARY

David said enter into his gates with thanksgiving and into his courts with praise. And when we enter into the gates, make a Joyful noise unto the Lord, we began to praise him. We began to be thankful we began to bless his Holy name, when I think of all his goodness and all God has done for me I have to praise him. Through our battles, our trails God is still Good, when we don't understand. And we ask the question why? God is still good. As we live for, Jesus we will experience the valley.

But Jesus promises to carry us through He promise to be with us, he promise never to leave us-Amen The sheep are completely dependent on the shepherd for provision guidance and protection. (John 10:11) Jesus tells us that he is the good shepherd, the good shepherd giveth his life for the sheep.

There will be storms in our life and sometime God will move them by saying them peace be still. And some time He will step on board and ride out the storm with us. God want us to wait on him for the right timing, have patients and faith. David told us why he had to wait on the Lord, that is where his salvation comes from. No one could deliver me all my hope is in God So many times when we are in the valley we pray for God to hurry up-get us out of this valley.

We don't like being in the valley, we want to shine from the mountain top, when we are in the valley, we learn how to be humble. Instead of David complaining he said I'm going to wait on the Lord, out of all David went through He never ask God Why. It takes good times and bad times to make a mature person life is a mixture of pain and pleasure, of victory and defeat of success and failure, of mountain tops and valleys.

Even in the darkest valleys our darkest days God is there with us. Valleys are going to happen only some are deeper than other, Valleys happen throughout life sometime one right after another. In (John 16) Jesus said in this word you will have trouble. It's not a matter of if I go in the valley, it is when I go in the valley. We are going to have difficulty times in this world. There will be times of suffering, sorrow, sickness, there will be times of frustration, it will happen, they are a normal part of life. Valleys will come they are unpredictable, have you noticed how easily a good day can become a bad day? (Matthew 5:45) The word tells us that it rains on the just and the unjust. This is not heaven, things are not perfect here on this earth, there are going to be some valleys in life. The valleys are temporary it not a permanent location.

David said even though I walk through the valley, if you never called on Jesus when you go through the valley you will call him. It not if I go through the valley, it's when I go through the valley. David said goodness and mercy shall follow me all the days of my life, and I will dwell in the house of the Lord forever. There are some deep dark valley's down here but don't get discouraged God is with you I don't know what kind of valley you might be going through but it only temporary.

Whatever your valley might be, God have all power, you might have to cry sometime, you may have to walk the floor in the middle night hours, go on press your way. If you never been in the valley, then you don't know what I am talking about. How are you going to tell me how to come through, when you never been there you never been in the valley. The valley is only temporary you can fine victory in the valley. Trials are only to test our faith, A prayer in the midst of hopelessness and depression. Our prayers should fit into what we know is consistent with God's character. (Psalm 143:10) Teach me to do thy will; for thou art my God: thy spirit is good; lead me into the land of uprightness.

A prayer for help when facing temptation. David asks God to protect him and to give him wisdom in accepting criticism. Be open to honest criticism-God may be speaking to you through others. A prayer when overwhelmed and desperate. When we feel cornered by our enemies, only God can keep us safe. Thanksgiving for answered prayer. God works out his plans for our lives and will bring us through the difficulties we face.

A very misunderstood concept throughout the religious world that it is extremely difficult to get God to answer prayer as all – much less answer all prayer. That is a lie of Satan and absolutely contrary to the Word of God. When you believe God's Word in your heart and you pray in line with His Word and have every right to expect your prayer to bring results. Jesus said; "Verily I say unto you, if ye have faith, and doubt not, ye shall not only do this which is done to the fig tree, but also if ye shall say unto this mountain. Be thou removed and be thou cast into the sea; it shall be done. And all things, whatsoever ye shall ask in prayer, believing, ye shall receive (Matthew 21:21-22). If God will answer the prayer of a sinner to be saved, he will certainly answer the prayers of born-again believers who come to him in faith concerning their lives. Jesus answered and said unto them. Verily I say unto you. If ye have faith, and doubt not, ye shall not do this which is done to the fig tree, but also if ye shall say unto this mountain. Be thou removed, and be thou cast into the sea; it shall be done.

When Peter cried out to Jesus, he answered him with one word: "Come," That command carried the authority necessary to defy all natural power. Faith supported him on the water Peter stepped out of the boat into a supernatural experience. When he swathe wind, however he became afraid and failed. He saw, he feared, and he sank.

(Jeremiah 33:3) God spoke to Jeremiah and said, "Call to me and I will answer you and tell you great and unsearchable things you do not know, This is not a promise only to one of the great prophets, (James 4:8) tells us to "come near to God and He will come near to you." Shadrach, Meshach, and Abednego were young witnesses to the awesome power of prayer. When faced with the fate of being thrown into a fiery furnace or bow down to King Nebuchadnezzar they chose the fiery furnace because they strongly believed in God and prayer.

If it be so, our God whom we serve is able to deliver us from the burning fiery furnace, and he will deliver us out of thine hand O king. Through their faith and belief in God, when He heard they call He delivered them and King Nebuchadnezzar became a believer and honored God.

(James 5:16) James said "The prayers of a righteous man is powerful and effective, Prayer can move mountains, if we have faith, Knowing how we should pray is important, but it is equally important to know when to pray. The answer to this is clearly and explicitly fined in (1Thessalonians 5:17) "Pray continually." The Holy Spirit is the great teacher of prayer, the Holy Spirit gathered the first followers of Jesus together in prayer. The Spirit taught them to remember Jesus, These and many others prayers in the Bible show us the character of God and help us know him more intimately. I began pondering, "What would someone think about God if they listened to me pray? Would they see him as trustworthy? Would they see that he is pure, holy and powerful?

Sometimes my prayers reflect a wishful faith that hope God is listening and will answer rather than a confident expectation that God will do what He would do. Think about this a man by the power of prayer shuts or opens the heavens, stops or brings down rain. He commands that a handful of flour and a little oil should suffice to feed several persons for several months, or perhaps even for more than a year, and it is fulfilled; breathes on a dead man, and restores him to life; bring down fire from heaven, to consume a sacrifice and an altar immersed in water. What can appear more extraordinary than this power of prayer?

God's Grace is another great witness to the power of God. Prayer is beneficial in all situations, its Praying Time, God is clearly stating the importance of prayer. He is letting us know we must communicate, simply talk to Him, we can talk to our Heavenly Father about anything at any time. Because the best witness to the power of God through prayer is YOU!

The Christian's most powerful resource is communion with God through prayer. The results are often greater than we thought were possible. Some people see prayer as a last resort to be tried all else fails. This is backwards. Prayer should come first. Since God's power is infinitely greater than our own, it only makes sense to rely on it especially because he encourages us to do so.

Many times, you go into prayer to ask God for help in one form or another. God said seek His kingdom and His righteousness and all the "STUFF" will be added. We don't have to worry about asking for all the materials we want all we have to do is turn from our wicked ways and seek God and His kingdom and you will receive the desires of your life. He wants us to cast upon Him; seek His face we do not have to worry about tomorrow He has it in control. Our heavenly father wants us to talk to Him. Jesus wants us to cast upon Him our every care. To know God is to have love. God wants us to love one another and pray for one another (1Thessalonias Ch 5: 16-17) Rejoice evermore. In every thing give thanks: for this is the will of God in Christ Jesus concerning you. Our joy, prayers, and thankfulness to God should not fluctuate with our circumstances or feelings. Obeying these three commands-rejoice. Keep on praying, and give thanks Prayer is the foundation for every successful endeavor in your life. It is a necessity for Christians to go before God and pray.

God hears prayers that are bold and confident in other words, pray effectively. Read and study God's Words that is the only way to get to know Him and know His will for your life. He said in His word that we Perish for the "Lack of knowledge. Do not pray in darkness, do not pray without knowing what to pray. Pray a fervent prayer, pray earnestly and let it be heart felt .

Our Father, which art in heaven, want to hear everything about us. It will not shock God for us to tell Him everything because He already knows it. He just wants us to trust in Him and talk to Him and ask for forgiveness. He loves us and wants to share in our pain and happiness. If we pray "right" we will get an answer to our prayers every time, in addition that answer is "YES."

When you pray use the name of Jesus, do not be afraid to call on the holy name of Jesus when you pray. The only way to get to the Father is through Jesus Christ. (John 14:6) Jesus saith him I am the way, the truth, and the life, no man cometh unto the Father, but by me.

When you don't know what to do, go to God's Word to see what He says about your particular situation then go before the Throne of Grace with confidence.

(2 Peter 3:9) The Lord is not slack concerning his promise, as some men count slackness; but is longsuffering to us-ward, not willing that any should perish, but that all should come to repentance.

Do not speak curses and blessings out the same fountain (mouth), Every time you say something negative about someone or a situation, you curse them. Have faith, confidence in what you say. We need confidence in our confidence in what you say. We need confidence in our confessions as well. If you lack confidence, meditate on the Holy Word of God. Meditate on the word until it speaks to you, forgive, communion and meditate. Faith is the law of God Faith seeds grow in your heart. Keep the weeds (doubt) out Knowing God's will, speaking God's Word is boldness in God's Word. When you know the word and believe the word and planet the Word in your heart you pray with confidence. However, if you do not know the Word of God when you pray, you do not have confidence or boldness. You are praying in fear, you are begging God. We do not have to beg God. He said in His Word that He stands at the door knocking and who let Him in, He will come in and sup with them.

Faith is one of the main ingredients in ones' prayer life many Christians do not know how to live by faith. For a Christians faith should be just as easy as breathing. You do not even have to think about how to breathe, you just do it. You are going to follow through with this no matter what. You cannot give up, you cannot cave in and you cannot quit.

God speaks to us because He desires to have fellowship with us. We are His most precious creation and He loves us dearly,

CHAPTER 9

NO CROSS NO CROWN

When I think of all his goodness and all he has done for me I have to give him glory, I got to praise him. We often wish we could escape troubles of this world, the pain, the loss, the sorrow, and the failure. If God didn't give us no rough roads to walk, if he didn't give us no mountains to climb. If he didn't give us no battles to fight, we wouldn't grow. Some time it takes trials and tribulations, to keep us humble. Some time it takes trials to keep up on our knees, down through this year somebody had some bad days and somebody had some good days. But thank God we are still here, God promises to carry us through He promise to be with us, He promise not to leaves us.

No Cross, No Crown everybody wants a crown, but nobody wants to bear there cross Jesus used this picture of his followers taking up their crosses to follow him. Following Jesus mean a true commitment no turning back to take up out cross and follow Jesus means to be willing to publicly identify with him. Be willing to face even suffering for his sake. Jesus said and he that taketh not his cross and follower after me is not worthy of me, is not worthy of me how much we love God can be measured by how well we treat other. Jesus tells us if we can nor bear out cross and come after him. We cannot be his disciple.

(Luke 9:23) If any man will come after me let him deny himself and take up his cross daily and follow me. We are committed daily to follow Jesus that choice determines our eternal destine. The cross of Christ is a symbol of suffering death, shame, rejection. When we as believers take up our cross and follow Jesus Christ we deny our own selves. We suffer in a lifelong battle against sin, the highest glory and privilege of any believer is to suffer for Christ and the gospel. Faith in Christ brings great blessing, but often great suffering God calls us to commitment not to comfort.

He promises to be with us through suffering and hardship not to spear us from them. Following Jesus mean total submission to him. No man having put his hand to the plough and looking back is fit for the kingdom of God. Jesus wants total dedication not halfhearted commitment. God desires to make us perfect and complete. Not to keep us from all pain instead of complaining about out struggles God is no respecter of person. What He done for me He will do for you, His promise does not mean we would not have trials and tribulations. It means that God himself will never leave us no matter what we face.

In order to get a crown we have got to bear our cross, there will be some battle to fight in this life. We wish we could escape troubles, the pains, The loss,

You remember that the Hem writer song an old Hem said Must Jesus beat the cross along, and all the world go free. No there is a cross for everyone and there is a cross for me. What every you are going through; God is right there by your side. Some time He will fix it and sometimes he will step on board with you and ride it out. There is nothing too hard for God, you remember he got into the Red Sea, He got into the Big Fish, He got into the Burning Brush one day, He got into the Lion Dens, He got into the fire furnaces, He got into the jail cell and it real and rock until the doors came open and souls was saved. Jesus got into the storm and the only thing he had to say PEACE BE STILL. When we are going through the storm of life he will get into it with us, all we have to do is hold on, press your way through, some time with tears in your eyes we must bear our Cross.

No Cross No Crown Whatever you are going through God is right there by your side, sometime he will fix it and sometime he will step on board with you and ride it out.

Jesus take Peter, James, and John with Him to the garden of Gethsemane told them to sit here watch for me while I go pray. Jesus went a little way fell on the ground cry out of my father if it be possible, let this cup pass from me, never the less not as I will but as thou wilt. Jesus prayed the same prayer two times, He went back to check on Peter, James and John they were sleeping, why couldn't you watch with me one hour? The spirit is willing but the flesh is weak, Jesus went back Prayed the third time my father if it possible let this cup pass from me, nevertheless not as I will but as thou will. No Cross No Crown God know when his children need help. He knows when the Load get to heavy, He know when the Road get to rough He sees you day after day toiling. The cross gets heavy some time, with pain in your body, just hold on, sometime you have to press your way. When you press call Jesus there is power in His name, Press call Jesus while you are pressing your way. David asked God to search for sin and point it out, even to the level of testing his thoughts. This is exploratory surgery for sin. How are we to recognize sin unless God points it out? Then when God shows us, we can repent, and repent and be forgiven. Make this verse your prayer. It you ask the Lord to search your prayer. If you ask the Lord to search your heart and your thoughts to reveal sin in your life, you will be continuing in God's everlasting way.

Have you ever felt that no one cared what happened to you? David had good reason to feel that way, and he wrote, "I cried unto thee, O LORD." Through prayer we can pull out of our tailspin and be reminded that God cares for us deeply. David was losing hope, caught in a deep depression that was paralyzing him with fear. At times, we feel caught in deepening depression, and we are unable to pull ourselves out. At those times, we can come to the Lord and, like David, express our true feelings. Then he will help us as we remember his miracles, reach out to him, trust him, and decide to do his will. David's prayer was for knowledge to do God's will, not his own. A prayer for guidance is self-centered if it doesn't recognize God's power to redirect our lives. Asking God to restructure our priorities awakens our minds and stirs our wills.

Set aside a special time and place to pray. You can pray more effectively if you have a special time and place for doing. So, the early morning or just before going to bed are good time to pray. It does not have to long- five minutes is a great start. It also helps if you have a routine please to pray in. it need not be a whole room a private corner in a bedroom or study will do. Ask God to help you with your prayer. God is not only able to answer your prayer, but he is also able to make your prayer to him stronger. You can also ask the Angels to help you pray.

Christians learn to pray through Jesus Christ who not only teachers us to pray, but also prayed himself. The Gospels are filled with examples of his prayer. Did Jesus himself have to learn to pray? Yes, he did true, he was the Son of God who know all things.

CHAPTER 10

THE BATTLEFIELD OF PRAYER

Every believer is invoiced in spiritual warfare, the problems we face are brought about by satanic forces principalities, powers, rulers of darkness of this world and wicked spirits in heavenly places. Our responsibility is to use the weapons of our warfare to fight the good fight of faith. What are those weapons? The name of Jesus, the Word of God, the Holy Spirit and the gifts of the spirit are major defense weapons on the battlefield of prayer.

Prayer is the battlefield, the time spent in prayer is the base of supply. The armor described in (Ephesians Ch. 6) is prayer armor. Your enemy is no other people, Satan is the source of all your trouble. Some people believe that God sends tribulation and trials. However, God has provided the weapons and armor that get us out of trouble! Satan is the troublemaker! God is not the trouble! Our neighbor is not the trouble! Our co-worker is not the problem!

Thank God, we have authority over Satan and his cohorts. We are to be strong in the Lord and in the power of his might. We must master our weapons and use them effectively. If we expect to win the war, we must spend the time to reinforce our troops through prayer. As a believer, you are a solder in the army of God. Visualize yourself standing ready for the battle with the armor of God protecting you—your lions grit with the truth. The breastplate of righteousness in the place.

Your feet are shod with the preparation pf the gospel of peace. ABOVE ALL, you are the shield of faith to quench all the fiery darts of the wicked. You have the helmet of salvation on your head and the sword of the Spirit—the Word of God -in your hand. The shield of faith is a vital part of the Christian's armor the shield of faith is a vital part of the Christian's armor. You are to put on the "whole armor of God," because the Christians life is warfare, a spiritual conflict. As Paul names the different parts of the Christian's armor, he comes to the shield and emphasizes its importance by saying, "About all, taking the shield of faith."

(Rom. 8:37) For with the shield of faith, nothing can hurt you;" in all these things we are more than conquerors through him who loved us." Prayer is an attitude it involves more than just making requests Prayer is communicating with God You can live in an attitude of prayer constantly, being in communion and fellowship with your heavenly Father every hour of the day.

In order to get results in prayer, you must be convinced of one basic fact: God wants to answer your prayers. In fact, he is as ready and willing to answer you, as he was to answer Jesus during his early ministry. This may be difficult for you to believe, but it is true.

I remember how amazed I was to learn about God's willingness to answer my prayers. I had always thought of myself as unworthy. I thought, why would God bother to answer my prayers? I realized the importance of the word of God, my attitude changed I realized that God does not see his children as unworthy. Notice how Jesus prayed:" that the world may know that thou hast sent me, and hast loved them, as thou hast loved me." Just think! God loves us as much as he loves Jesus! We are worthy.

God's word is His will, when you pray in line with the Word, you have automatically prayed in line with God's will.(1 John 5:14-15) says, and this is the confidence that we have in him if we ask any thing according to his will, he heareth us. And if we know that he hears us.

We have to remember that the Lord does not always want to change our circumstances. God wants to change our character. The ways He changes out character are through the things that happen to us. We are changed through out decisions-particularly during the toughest trials-to align ourselves with the world or to align ourselves with Him. Sometimes it seem like God does not hear us when we pray, but don't give up, keep praying keep the faith, believe and trust Him, never give up on Jesus. He didn't give up on you, so don't you give up on Him. If we line up with God's word, pray in faith, believe and go on and thank God for whatever you ask Him for. Believing it is done.

You have to learn how to speak to your problems. When you pray do not have doubt in your heart, we have got to believe that it is done. Jesus tells us in (Mark 11:24) "Therefore I say to you, whatever things you ask when you pray, believe that you receive them, and you will have them. Many times just before God blesses us, He will stand back, and let the Devil put a mountain in our life, Just to see if you can come through without doubting.

You do not learn faith when you have lots of money, You learn faith when your money runs very short, and you need to pay a bill. You do not learn faith when you are feeling good in the body. You learn faith when your body is racking with pains. When you can say, "Thu He slay me, yet shall I trust him." When you pray in His name, He will answer. However, let me remind you, there are two requirements for answers to prayer.

FIRST: We are to abide in Him (Jesus) that is to continue in Him. Stay in His perfect will at all cost.

SECOND: His words are to abide in us, the words are to become a part of our life you may say, I have prayed, and God has not answered me.

Sometime the answer is delayed but not denied-delay according to His will. The resurrection of Lazarus is a good example of delayed answer to prayer. Sometime the answer is immediately, He answers Peter immediately. And sometime the answer is no, but when God answer with a No, He always accompanies the answer with PEACE and GRACE.

Many time the answers is sometime different from what we expect, we pray for perseverance and God send tribulation, because tribulation produces perseverance. (Psalm 40:1) I waited patiently for the Lord; he turned to me and heard my cry. If we line with God's Word, pray in faith, believe and go on and thank God for whatever you ask him for Believing it is done.

You have to learn how to speak to your problems, When you pray do not have doubt in your heart, we have got to believe that it is done. Jesus tells us in (Mark 11:24), "Therefore I say to You, whatever things you ask when you pray, believe that you receive them, and you will have them. Many times just before God blesses us, He will stand back, and let the Devil put a mountain in our life. Just to see if you can come through without doubting.

Waiting for God to help us is not easy, but David received four benefits from waiting (1) God lifted him out of his despair,(2) God set his feet on firm ground, (3) God established his goings (steadied him as he walked), and(4) God gave him a new song. Often blessings cannot be received unless we go through the trial of waiting.

Concerning this thing, I pleaded with the Lord three times that it might depart from me. In addition, He said to me, "My Grace is sufficient for you, for strength is made perfect in weakness." Therefore, most gladly I will rather boast in my infirmities, that the power of Christ may rest upon me.

We know God answers prayers, but there are times we want Him to answer on our time and not His, When we're impatient we lose faith that He will answer our prayer, so we try to take matters into our own hands. We try to control our lives. We need to have faith that He will provide for us because He loves us. God answers all our prayers, not according to our wishes, but according to His Perfect will.

I was raise up from a child praying and believing that God would answer my prayers. I believe like (Daniel 3:17-18). "If that is the case, Our God whom we serve is able to deliver us from the burning fiery furnace, and He will Deliver us from your hands, O king. "But if not, let it be knows to you, O king, that we do not serve your gods, nor will we worship the gold image, which you have set up.

We are living in a world that is weak in prayer, Our leaders are weak in prayer. Many people make time for everything except God. Until they want God to do something for them. Then that is when we fine time, and when God answer our prayers, we forget about Him and go back to our evil ways. Covid 19 hit many people prayer list, and yet after God brought us through, God is on the backburner again. Through the floods, and through the storms everybody calling on Jesus, when He brings us through, we put Him on the back burner until we need Him again.

(Psalm 46:1-3) God is our refuge and strength, and ever present help in trouble. Therefore we will not fear, though the though its waters roar and foam the mountains quake with their surging. God speaks to us because He desires to have fellowship with us. We are His most precious creation and He loves us dearly. Every one of us is a child of God. God knows that we constantly need direction in our travels through life. God also realizes we need comfort and assurance in order to get through all the trials and tribulations of this mean and cruel world. God wants us to get to know Him.

God speaks to us through His Word, He uses the Bible as His foremost tool to impart truth. He speaks through the Holy Spirit who is with us every second of the day. God speaks to us through other believers, God speaks to us through divine circumstances, We are all living under heavenly guidance, and if you look closely, you will see the hand of God written upon many of the wonderful things that come into your life.

(Romans 6:23) For the wages of sin is death; but the gift of God is eternal life through Jesus Christ our Lord. You are free to choose between two masters, but you are not free to adjust the consequences of your choice. Each of the two masters pays with his own kind of currency. The currency of sin is eternal death. That is all you can expect or hope for in life without God. Christ's currency is eternal life-new life with God that begins on earth and continues forever with God. What choice have you made? (Romans 1:4) and declared to be the Son of God with power according to the spirit of holiness by the resurrection from the dead. Paul states that Jesus is the Son of God, the promised Messiah, and the resurrected Lord. Paul called Jesus a descendant of King David ("of the seed of David") to emphasize that Jesus truly fulfilled the Old Testament Scriptures predicting that the Messiah would come from David's line. With this statement of faith, Paul declared his agreement with the teaching of all Scripture and of the apostles.

Here Paul also summarizes the Good News about Jesus Christ who (1) came as a human ("according to the flesh" means by natural descent), (2) was part of the jewish royal line through David, (3) died and was raised from the dead, and (4) opened the door for God's kindness to be poured out on us. The book of Romans is an expansion of these themes. When you pray continually about a concern, don't be surprised at how God answers. Paul prayed to visit Rome so he could teach the Christians there. When the finally arrived in Rome. It was as a prisoner. Paul prayed for a safe trip, and he did arrive safely-after getting arrested, slapped in the face, shipwrecked, and bitten by a poisonous snake. When you sincerely pray, God will answer-although sometimes in timing and in ways you do not expect. (John 3:16) For God so loved the world, that he gave his only begotten Son, that whosoever believeth in him should not perish, but have everlasting life.

The entire Gospel comes into focus in this verse. God's love is not static or self-centered; it reaches out and draws others in. Here God sets the pattern of true love, the basis for all love relationships-when you love someone dearly, you are willing to give freely to the point of self-sacrifice. God paid dearly with the life of his Son, the highest price he could pay. Jesus accepted our punishment, paid the price for our sins, and then offered us the new life he had bought for us. When we share the Gospel with others, our love must be like Jesus'-willingly giving up our own comfort and security so that others might join us in receiving God love.

When we share the Gospel with others, our love must be like Jesus'-willingly giving up our own comfort and security so that others might join us in receiving God's love. (Jeremiah 33:3) Call unto me, and I will answer thee, and shew thew thee great and mighty things, which thou knowest not. God assures Jeremiah that he has only to ask, God is ready to answer our prayers but we must ask for his assistance. Surely he could take care of our needs without our asking. But when we ask, we are acknowledging that he alone is God and that we cannot accomplish in our own strength all that is his domain to do. When we ask, we must humble ourselves. Lay aside our willfulness and worry, and determine to obey him.

Jesus, our example, once prayed, "All things are possible unto thee nevertheless not what I will, but what thou wilt." Our prayers are often motivated by our own interests and desires. We like to hear that we can have anything. But Jesus prayed with God's interests in mind. When we pray, we can express our desires, but we should want his will above ours. Check yourself to see if your prayers focus on your interests or God's.

(James 5:16) Confess your faults one to another, and pray one for another, that ye may be healed. The effectual fervent prayer of a righteous man availeth much. The Christian's most powerful resource is communion with God through prayer. The results are often greater than we thought were possible. Some people see prayer as a last resort to be tried when all else fails. This is backwards. Prayer should come first. Since God's power is infinitely greater than our own, it only makes sense to rely on it-especially because he encourages us to do so.

"The prayer of faith" does not refer to the faith of the sick person, but to the faith of the people praying. God heals, faith doesn't and all prayers are subject to God's will but our prayers are part of God's healing process. "Confess your faults" can be translated "confess your sins." Christ has made it possible for us to go directly to God for forgiveness, but confessing our sins to one another still has an important place in the life of the church. (1) If we have sinned against an individual, we must ask him or her to forgive us. (2) If our has sin affected the church, we must confess it publicly. (3) If we need loving support as we struggle with a sin, we should confess it to those who are able to provide that support. (4) If after confessing a private sin to God, we still don't feel his forgiveness, we may wish to confess that sin to a fellow believer and hear him or her assure us of God's pardon. In Christ's Kingdom, every believer is a priest to other believers. We must help others come to Christ and tell them that He will forgive them, because He loves us and want us to be his children.

CHAPTER 11

THE POWER OF PRAYER

(Psalm 55:17) Evening, and morning, and at noon, will I pray, and cry aloud: and he shall hear my voice. Praying morning, noon, and night is certainly an excellent way to maintain correct priorities throughout every day. (Daniel 6:10) Now when Daniel knew that the writing was signed, he went into his house; and his windows being open in his chamber toward Jerusalem, he kneeled upon his knees three times a day, and prayed, and gave thanks before his God, as he did. Although Daniel knew about the law against praying to anyone except the king, he still prayed three times a day as he always had. Daniel had a disciplined prayer life. Our prayers are usually interrupted not by threats or pressures cut into your prayer time. Pray regularly, no matter what.

God has ways of delivering his people that none of us can imagine. It is always premature to give up and give in to the pressure of unbelievers, because God has power they know nothing about GOD CAN SHUT THE LIONS' MOUTHS. The person who trusts in God and obey his will is untouchable until God takes him or her. To trust God is to have immeasurable peace, God who deliver Daniel, will deliver you. Do you trust him with your life?

(1 Chronicles 29:19) And give unto Solomon my son a perfect heart, to keep thy commandments, thy testimonies, and thy statutes, and to

do all these things, and to build the palace, for which I have made provision. A "perfect" heart means a heart that is entirely dedicated to God. This is what David prayed for Solomon-a heart that desired, above all else, to serve God. Do you find it hard to do what God want, Or even harder to want, or even harder to want do it? God can give you a perfect heart. If you believe in Jesus Christ, this is already happening in you. Paul wrote that God works within us "both to will and to do of his good pleasure" Consider yourself blessed if someone in your life is praying this way for you.

We too have the remarkable privilege to faithfully pray for the people God has placed in our lives. Our example of faithfulness can make an indelible impact that will remain even after we're gone. Just as God continued to work out the answers to David's prayers for Solomon and Israel after he was gone, so too the impact of our prayers outlives us. (John 14:6) Jesus saith unto him, I am the way, the truth, and the life: no man cometh unto the Father; but by me. This is one of the most basic and important passages in Scripture. How can we know the way to God? Only through Jesus. Jesus is the way because he is both God and man.

By uniting our lives with us, we are united with God. Trust Jesus to take you to the Father, and all the benefits of being God's child will be yours. Jesus says he is the only way to the God the Father. Some people may argue that is too narrow. In reality, it is wide enough for the whole world, if the world chooses to accept it. Instead of worrying about how limited it sounds to have only one way, we should be saying, "Thank you, God, for providing a sure way to get you!"

As the way, Jesus is out path to the Father. As the truth, he is the reality of all God's promises. As the life, he joins his divine life to ours, both now and eternally. Jesus is, in truth, the only living way to the Father. (John 14:34) A new commandment I give unto you, That ye love one another; as I have love you, that ye also love one another. To love others was not a new commandment but to love others as much as Christ loved others was revolutionary. Now we are to love others based on Jesus' sacrificial love for us. Such love will not only bring unbelievers to Christ, it will also keep believers strong and united in a world hostile to God. Jesus was a loving example of Jesus' love.

Jesus says that our Christlike love will show we are his disciples. Do people see petty bickering, jealousy, and division in your church? Or do they know you are Jesus' followers by your love for one another? Love is more than simply warm feeling; it is an attitude that reveals itself in action. How can we love others as Jesus loves us? By helping when it's not convenient, by giving when it hurts, by devoting energy to others' welfare rather than our own, by absorbing hurts from others without complaining of fighting back. This kind of love is hard to do. That is why people notice when you do it and know you are empowered by a supernatural source. The Bible has another beautiful description of love.

Love is more important than all the spiritual gifts exercised in the church body. Great faith, acts of dedication or sacrifice, and miracle-working power produce very little without love. Love makes our actions and gifts useful. Although people have different gifts, love available to everyone.

(1 John 1:5-6) This then is the message which we have heard of him, and declare unto you, that God is light, and in him is no darkness at all. If we say that we have fellowship with him, and walk in darkness, we lie, and do not the truth: Light represents what is good, pure, true, holy, and reliable. Darkness represents sin and evil. To say "God is light" means that God is perfectly holy and true, and that he alone can guide us out of the darkness of sin. Light is also related to truth, in that it exposes whatever exists, whether it is good or bad. In the dark, good and evil look alike, in the light, they can be clearly distinguished. Just as darkness cannot exist in the presence of light, sin cannot exist in the presence of a holy God. If we want to have a relationship with

God, we must put aside our sinful ways of living. To claim that we belong to him but then to live for ourselves is hypocrisy. Christ will expose and judge such deceit.

God drew near to us through Jesus so we could know Him personally and be with Him forever. His loving presence with us is the greatest gift of all. No one can claim to be a Christian and still live and immorality. We can't love God and court sin at the same time. Jesus' blood cleanse us from every sin? Real cleansing from sin came with Jesus, the "Lamb of God, which taketh away the sin of the world." Sin, by its very nature, brings death-that is a fact as certain as the law of gravity. Jesus did not die for his own sins; he had none. Instead. By a transaction we may never fully understand, he died for the sins of the world.

When we commit our life to Christ and thus identify ourselves with him, his death becomes ours. He has paid the penalty for our sins; his blood has cleansed us just as he rose from the grave, we rise to a new life of fellowship with him. (Philippians 2:6) Who being in the form of God thought it not robbery to be equal with God. (1) He has always existed with God,(2) he is equal to God because he is God, (3) though he is God, he became man In order to fulfill God's plan of salvation for all people, (4) he did not just pretend to have a man's body-he actually became a man to identity with msn's sins,(5) he voluntarily laid aside his divine rights ad privileges out of love for his Father, (6) he died on the cross for our sins, so we wouldn't have to face eternal death;(7) God glorified him because of his obedience; (8) God raised him to his original position all the Father's right hand where he will reign forever as our Lord and judge.

(Philippians 4:6-7) Be careful for nothing; but in everything by prayer and supplication with thanksgiving let your requests be made known unto God. And the peace of God, which passeth all understanding, shall keep your hearts and minds through Christ Jesus. I learned to" be careful for nothing" don't worry, imagine never worrying about anything! It seems like an impossibility we all have worries on the job, in our homes, at school. But Paul's advice is to turn your worries into prayers. Do you want to worry less? If so then, pray more! Whenever you start to worry, Stop and pray. Just take everything too God in pray, you will feel better. Satan want you to worry,(Revelation 12:9) And the great dragon was cast out, that old serpent, called the Devil, and Satan, which deceiveth the whole world; he was cast out into the earth, and his angels were cast out with him. Satan is not just a symbol or legend; he is very, very real. Some people think he is just an angle. Yes when he was in heaven he was a good angle, until day he wanted to be like God, He wanted to take over.

He is very real, originally he was an angel of God, but through his pride, he became corrupt. Satan is God's enemy and he constantly tries to hinder God's work but he is limited by God's power and can do only what he is permitted to do. The name Satan mean "Adversary" or "Accuser." He is very actively look for people to attack. He love to try to attack, He likes to seek out believers who are vulnerable in their faith, who are spiritually weak, or who are isolated from other believers.

Even though God permits Satan to do his work in this word, God is still in control. And Jesus has complete power over Satan-he defeated Satan when he died and rose again for the sins of mankind. One day Satan will be bound forever, never again to do his evil work. We don't have to worry about anything, have FAITH in God(Mark 11:22-23-24) And Jesus answering saith unto them, Have faith in God, For verily I say unto you, That whosoever shall say unto this mountain, Be thou removed, and be thou cast into the sea; and shall not doubt in his heart, but shall believe that those things which he saith shall come to pass; he shall have whatsoever he saith. Therefore I say unto you, What things soever ye desire, when ye pray, believe that ye receive them, and ye shall have them. The kind of prayer that moves mountains is prayer for the fruitfulness of God's Kingdom. It would seem impossible to move a mountain into the sea, so Jesus used that picture to show that God can do anything. God will answer your prayers, but not as a result of your positive mental attitude. Other conditions must be met: (1) You must be a believe, (2) you must not hold a grudge against another person (3) you must not pray with selfish motives, (4) Your request must be for the good of his kingdom, To pray effectively, you need faith in God, not faith in the object of your request. If you focus only on you request, you will be left with nothing if your request is refused.

Jesus our example, once prayed, "All things are possible unto thee; nevertheless not what I will, but what thou wilt" Our prayers are often motivated by our own interests and desires. We like to hear that we can have anything. But Jesus prayed with God's interests in mind. When we pray, we can express our we should want his will above ours. Check yourself to see if your prayers focus on your interests or God's.

CHAPTER 12

WHAT IS PRAY

Prayer is a conversation of the heart with God. Through prayer we align *ourselves with our Creator, and His presence is revealed to us. We grow in our love and* worship of Him. And when we are united with our Lord through prayer, our life becomes fuller, richer, and more joyous. Prayer is a cleaning process, washing our thoughts, feelings, motives, and will, purifying the entire being including

"Prayer is the key of the morning and the bolt of the evening. There is no peace without the grace of God, and there is no grace of God without prayer. Many people feel profoundly calm after praying. Prayer is deeply relaxing, and those who do it regularly are, in effect, meditating. But science cannot explain some remarkable studies showing that to a degree that goes way beyond coincidence, prayer works.

Prayer is what you do when you're done struggling with a problem, and you're ready to call forth its solution. Prayer is not about trying to get God to do something to you or give something to you. Its about allowing God to do something through you.

Having a spirit prayer is one of the most important things in our walk with Christ. We must be meditative and contemplatives, listening to Him speak. When we do this, our life is changed. When we pray in the Spirit, we are in prayer in our whole life, no just our "prayer" time.

We are praying as we work, as we play, as we spend time alone and as we spend time with friends and family.

"A good prayer life, in my estimation, is being aware of God's presence and being transparent with Him about what I am experiencing," says Dr. Dennis Cox of New Port Richey, Fla. "Sometimes involves a formal audible prayer, but more often it is a thought life that is shared with God."

I heard a pastor in Clearwater, Fla.; recently talk about our godly relationships. He said the only thing we'll be judged on is how we relate to others on a godly basis. We need to ask ourselves whether our relationships at work and at home are godly. Prayer helps us examine our relationship with our Creator and helps us focus our relationship with others so they indeed are godly.

For prayer helps us know the heart of our Lord and His desires for our life. I heard an interesting statement: "We see what we are programmed to see." In other words, we set our minds so we get out of things only what we want to get out of them.

But when we are constantly seeking our Lord in prayer, we align ourselves with His wishes and desires. We are no longer programmed to see what we want, but we see what God wants. We turn over control of our life to Him and do His will. In prayer we pour out to Him our joys, our anguish and petitions for ourselves and others. And by faith we know He hears and responds to our cries.

"Prayer must have priority. Prayer must be our bolt to lock up the night, our key to open the day." Prayer is the single most important thing we can do to know God, to be in union with Him. If we don't have a good prayer life, our priorities get mixed up. If we neglect our prayer life, we lose sight of our Lord, and we become proud and arrogant people who think we don't need God. Prayer, therefore, sets us straight and keeps us safe in our Lord.

The Lord is my rock, my fortress and my deliverer; my God is my rock, in whom I take refuge. He is my shield and the light of my salvation, my stronghold. Psalm 18:2

How we view God and pray to Him indicates where our priorities are and whether we have the privilege of realizing that God belongs above and ahead of everything.

Prayer exerts unbelievable demands on us. As we open our heart and allow the Lord to rule our life, He will develop us in ways far beyond anything we, on our own, have ever attempted. Worshipful prayer transcends the structure of ingrained behavior and rigid church traditions. In prayer we can experience the holy and compassionate heart of the Lord.

The essence of praying as we should is spelled out in Matthew 22:34-40: *Hearing that Jesus had silenced the Sadducees, the Pharisees got together. One of them, an expert in the law, tested him with this question: "Teacher, which is the greatest commandment in the Law?" Jesus replied: "Love the Lord your God with all your heart and with all your soul and with all your mind. This is the first and greatest commandment. And the second is like it: 'Love your neighbor as yourself.' All the Law and the Prophets hang on these two commandments."*

Our Lord commands a relationship of love with Him, reflected in our prayer life. Without love, our prayer is meaningless, a series of empty words. Without love, our walk with God is a ritual. Without love, we cannot truly know and worship Him. But when we approach God in love, our prayer is a rich, full experience. He seeks a relationship of love and adoration so we can talk together and have Him with us at all time.

The first side of the triangle is intimacy, or "knowing." in both Hebrew and Greek, "to know" implies and intimate relationship best seen in a very close friendship. It is a relationship that takes time and effort.

An intimate relationship is built and strengthened by sharing ideas and experiences, by support, communication

To become intimate with God, we need to know the Word and the person of Jesus Christ. If we're just acquainted with Him, we know about the God of creation, but we certainly don't love Him. It is merely an awareness of someone one we don't know on an intimate basis. To "know" God, we need to study His Word faithfully on a regular basis and to seek his true blessings on us in His intimacy. We then know His will for our lives and can turn to Him in rimes of trouble as well as in times of joy.

The second side is our commitment to Him. Commitment provides the reliable strength necessary for the relationship to survive the ups and downs of our life on Earth. It's where the decision to love and maintain love is made. Commitment will grow or wither depending on how it is nurtured.

Proverbs 16:3 says, "Commit to the Lord whatever you do, and your plans will succeed." One way we help commitment grow is by staying focused on God through prayer. As Psalm 34:1 says, "I will extol the Lord at all times; his praise will always be on my lips."

But we must make sure we're committed to more than the habit of prayer. We must seek to be focused, fervent and faithful in our relationship to our Redeemer. The third side in our relationship of love with God is passion. Romance and physical union between husband and wife are essential components for fulfilling love. Passion makes their desire to be united. And passion motivates them to greater commitment and leads to deeper intimacy with one another.

Just as passion cements their relationship, so it should seal our relationship wit God. We should pray deeply and passionately, making God our highest priority, above all other concerns and desires. This passion motivates us to put Him first. In my life as a minister, having passion for the Lord and compassion for my patients go hand in hand. I have failed in this pursuit many times, and the Lord in His mercy repeatedly has shown me that my compassion for patients must come from the passion I have for Him.

All three facets of the love relationship play a vital rile in our prayer life. If they are balanced and work together, our lives are focused on God, and we have set Him as the highest priority. We know Him and study His Word, we are committed to a life of prayer, and we pray fervently, not as a task to be accomplished but because we desire a closer relationship with Him. We know God and we love Him. That really determines whether we pray to Him. We want to align ourselves with our Creator and put Him as our highest priority, far above the material things of this world.

That's not to say life will be easy even when we are focused on the Lord through prayer. We still will face problems, frustrations and difficult times. But some of the most difficult events in our lives are meant to help us rely on God. Just as Calvary was the worst day in the world, it also was the best day. Our worst events will make us the strongest, because when we rely on the Lord instead of collapsing we turn all our attention to Him and not to ourselves. We seek God's way, rather than our own.

Even though we are assured so many blessings through our relationship with our Lord in prayer, we still struggle to do it. Prayer is not a natural thing. It is easier to contribute time or money then to pray and to pray unceasingly.

Prayer also interferes with our ambitions and our own agendas. It forces us to surrender our independence and submit to God. The only thing He asks of us is to trust in His grace and then to grow closer to Him. It sounds simple, but living that commitment every day requires constant dedication. God renews and renourishes that commitment in us through our contact with him in prayer.

Some days, when complications pile up or my schedule gets bogged down, I question the purpose of my work. Prayer is the only way out of those dark situations. When I remember that the only work that makes a difference is the work that is done for the Lord, I am reminded of my need to turn to Him.

We know that prayer reveals the heart of God, that we have a relationship of love reflected in our prayer and that, even though we face problems and don't feel like praying, Prayer is essential. We need presence of God in our lives, and prayer helps us align ourselves with Him.

There are three stages we go through in our prayer that help show us the purpose of prayer.

They help build our relationship of love with our Lord so we see Him not as some divine "Santa Claus" but as a Father who loves us and wants us aligned with Him.

The Lord is my light and my salvation – whom shall I fear? The Lord is the stronghold of my life – of whom shall I be afraid? Psalm 27:1

First, in our prayer we should honor God. Word, says, "Prayer is an act of worship, a paying homage" to our Father in heaven. The Scriptures are full of verses show us how to honor God, how to worship and praise Him.

Prayer cannot be successfully separated from worship, for it prepares the soul for worship, expresses the spirit in worship and interacts with god, which is worship. Worship without prayer is like daytime without light, a school without students, a choir without music or an automobile without fuel; the praying saint cannot keep from worshiping; the prayerless saint cannot rise to worship.

Judson Cornwell

We must get serious about worship if we want a lifestyle of prayer. How can we pray to God if we don't first acknowledge Him as our Redeemer and Lord? In worship, as in prayer, we align ourselves with God.

Second, through prayer we become "inclined to God," humbling ourselves so we become totally dependent on Him and we seek His will in all we do every day and in every decision of our lives.

A lifestyle of prayer leads us to the realization that, without Him, we can do nothing of lasting value. The apostle Paul recognized his helplessness without God, writing in Romans 7:18, "I know that nothing good lives in me, that is, in my sinful nature. For I have the desire to do what is good, but I cannot carry it out."

When we're not in touch with God through prayer, we think we can take care of ourselves when we can't. We think we're independent and in control our lives. Those times when I'm too busy to pray, the wheel falls off my car. Soon, I'm spinning toward a crash. Life ceases to be a joy. We need the Lord more than we realize. James 4:10 says, "Humble yourselves before the Lord, and he will lift you up."

By making God our highest priority, we acknowledge that He is in control and that we want to align ourselves with Him in every decision we make and every action we take.

Seek ye first the Kingdom of God and His Righteousness.
Matthew 6:33

Every time we do something, we have a choice. We have a choice to do it as the world does it, or to do it as the Lord Jesus would have us do it. In prayer we discover what He wants us to do. We learn to open ourselves to Him, seeking His will, and to depend on His guidance and love.

The worst thing I can do as a pastor is seek applause and acceptance men rather than seeking to please God. It is far easier for pastors with large churches to worship the rewards, financially and emotionally, from our members. It's tempting to want to be worshiped as a pastor and to worship the job rather than worship the Lord. Instead, the challenge, the struggle, is to want to serve Jesus through our surrender to His will. Then we can serve others with humility and an attitude of caring and love.

> *Ask, and it will be given to you; seek and you will find; knock and the door will be opened to you. For everyone who asks receives; he who seeks finds; and to him who knocks, the door will be opened.*
> *Matthew 7:7-8*

> *You may ask me for anything in my name, and I will do it.*
> *John 14:14*

The third reason for prayer is so we may receive what we need from God. He gives us what we need, in line with His character. When we ask of God in the name of Jesus, we pray for the same things He desires to give us, as outlined in His Word.

Prayer, therefore, involves agreeing with God – being aligned with Him. We direct our prayers toward the accomplishment of His purposes in this world. Praying God's promises ensures victory and God's blessings upon us.

> *"For I know the plans I have for you, "declares the Lord, :plans to prosper you and not to harm you, plans to give you hope and a future, then you will call upon me and come and pray to me, and I will listen to you. You will seek me and find me when you seek me with all your heart."*
> *Jeremiah 29: 11-13*

Prayer helps us make sure we are constantly focused on our Redeemer and Lord. Our prayer as Christians should be to seek to be with Christ, worshiping Him on the cross. It should be faithful, fervent and focused, consuming all the facets of our life. Our job is to integrate our whole life with Christ – our work, our play, and our families – so that everything we do, every choice we make, is based on our subconscious awareness of the person of Jesus Christ.

A life or prayer develops the life of God in each of us; it doesn't develop our selves or promote our motives. But it does change us as we came closer to Him. We grow more dependent on God, more faithful to Him, and love Him and others more as we spend more time in prayer.

We today yearn for prayer and hide from prayer. We are attracted to it and repelled by it. We believe prayer is something we should do, even something we want to do, but it seems like a chasm stands between us and actually praying. We experience the agony of prayerlessness.

We are not quite sure what holds us back, of course we are busy with work and family obligations, but that is only a smoke screen. Our busyness seldom keeps us from eating or sleeping or making love. No, there is something deeper, more profound keeping us in check. In reality, there are any number of "something's" preventing us, all of which we will explore in due time. But for now, there is one "something" that needs immediate attention. It is the notion – all most universal among us modern high achievers – that we have to have everything "just right" in order to pray. That is, before we can really pray, our lives need some fine tuning, or we need to know more about how to pray, or we need to study the philosophical questions surrounding prayer, or we need to have a better grasp of the great traditions of prayer. And on it goes. It isn't that these are wrong concerns or that there is never a time to deal with them. But we are starting from the wrong end of things – putting the cart before the horse. Our problem is that we assume prayer is something to master the way we master algebra or unto mechanics. That puts us in the "on-top" position, where we are competent and in control. But when praying, we come "underneath," where we calmly and deliberately surrender control and become incompetent, "To pray".

I used to think that I needed to get all my motives straightened out before I could pray. I would be in some prayer group, for example, and I would examine what I had just prayed and think to myself, "How utterly foolish and self-centered; I can't pray this way!" And so I would determine never to pray again until my motives were pure. You understand, I did not want to be a hypocrite. I knew that God is holy and righteous. I knew that prayer is no magic incantation. I knew that I must use God for my own ends. But the practical effect of all this internal soul-searching was to completely paralyze my ability to pray.

The truth of the matter is, we all come to prayer with a tangled mass of motives – altruistic and selfish, merciful and hateful, loving and bitter. Frankly, this side of eternity we will never unravel the good from the bad, the pure from the impure. But what I have come to see is that God is big enough to receive us with all our mixture. We do not have to be bright, or pure, or filled with faith, or anything. That is what grace means, and not only are we saved by grace, we live by it as well. And we pray by it.

Jesus reminds us that prayer is a little like children coming to their parents. Our children come to us with the craziest requests at times! often we are grieved by the meanness and selfishness in their requests, but we would be all the more grieved if they never came to us even with their meanness and selfishness. We are simply glad that they do come – mixed motives and all.

This is precisely how it is with prayer. We will never have pure enough motives, or be good enough, or know enough in order to pray rightly. We simply must set all these thing aside and begin praying. In fact, it is in the very act of prayer itself – the intimate, on –going interaction with God – that matters are cared for in due time.

What I am trying to say is that God receives us just as we are and accepts our prayers just as they are. In the same way that a small child cannot draw a bad picture so a child of God cannot offer a bad prayer, so we are brought to the most basic, the most primary form of prayer: Simple Prayer. Let me describe it for you. In Simple Prayer we bring ourselves before God just as we are, warts and all. Like children before a loving father, we open our hearts and make our requests. We do not try sort things out, the good from the bad. We simply and unpretentiously share our concerns and make our petitions. We tell God, for example, how frustrated we are with the co-worker at the office or the neighbor down the street. We ask for food, favorable weather, and good health.

In a very real sense we are the focus of Simple Prayer. Our needs, our wants, our concerns dominate our prayer experience. Our prayers are shot through with plenty of pride, conceit, vanity, pretentiousness, haughtiness, and general all-round egocentricity. No doubt there are also magnanimity, generosity, unselfishness, and universal goodwill.

We make mistakes – lots of them; we sin; we fall down. Often – but each time we get up and begin again. We pray again. We seek to follow God again. And again our insolence and self-indulgence defeat us. Never mind. We confess and begin again . . . and again . . . and again. In fact, sometimes Simple Prayer is called the Prayer of Beginning Again."

Simple Prayer is the most common form of prayer in the Bible. There is little that is lofty or magnanimous about the faith heroes who journey across the pages of Scripture. Think of Moses complaining to God about his stiff-necked and erstwhile followers: "Why have I not found favor in your sight, that you lay the burden of all this people on me? Did I conceive all this people? Did I give birth to them, that you should say to me, 'Carry them in your bosom, as a nurse carries a sucking child,' to the land that you promised on oath to their ancestors?" (Num. 11:11b-12).

Simple Prayer is found throughout Scripture. Abraham prayed this way, as did Joseph, Joshua, Hannah, David, Gideon, Ruth, Peter, James, John, and a host of other biblical luminaries.

Simple Prayer involves ordinary people bringing ordinary concerns to a loving compassionate Father. There is no pretense in Simple Prayer. We do not pretend to be more holy, more pure, or more saintly we actually are. We do not try to conceal our conflicting and contradictory motives from God – or ourselves. And in this posture we pour out our heart to the God who is greater then our heart and who knows all things

(1 John 3:20).

Simple Prayer is beginning prayer. It is the prayer of children, and yet we will return to it again and again. Saint Teresa of Avila notes, "There is no stage of prayer so sublime that it isn't necessary to return often to the beginning." Jesus, for example, calls us to Simple Prayer when he urges us to ask for daily bread. As John Dalrymple rightly observes, "We never outgrow this kind of prayer, because we never outgrow the needs which give rise to it."

There is a temptation, especially by the "sophisticated," to despise this most elementary way of praying. They seek to skip over Simple Prayer in the hopes of advancing to more "mature" expressions of prayer. They smile at the egotistical asking, asking, asking of so many. Grandly they speak of avoiding "self-centered prayer in favor of "other –centered prayer." What these people fail to see, however, is that Simple Prayer is necessary, even essential, to the spiritual life. The only way we move beyond "self – centered prayer" (if indeed we ever do) is by going through it, not by making a detour around it.

Those who think they can leap over Simple Prayer deceive themselves. Most likely they themselves have not prayed. They may have discussed prayer, analyzed prayer, even written books about prayer, but it is highly unlikely that they have actually prayed.

But when we pray, genuinely pray, the real condition of our heart is revealed. This is as it should be. This is when God truly begins to work with us.

Up to this point we have been describing Simple Prayer. That is theory. But we must move beyond theory to ask the question for which all that has gone before is prelude. How do we practice Simple Prayer? What do we do? Where do we begin?

Very simply, we begin right where we are: in our families, on our jobs, with our neighbors and friends. Now, I wish this did not sound so trivial, because, on the practical level of knowing God, it is the most profound truth we will ever hear. To believe that God can reach us and bless us in the ordinary junctures of daily life is the stuff of prayer. But we want to throw this away, so hard is it for us to believe that God would enter our space. "God can't bless me here," we moan, "When I graduate . . ." "When I'm the chairman of the board . . ." "When I'm the president of the company . . ." "When I'm the senior pastor . . . then God can bless me." But you see, the only place God can bless us is right where we are, because that is the only place we are!

Do you remember Moses at the burning bush? God had to tell him to take off his shoes – he did not know he was on holy ground. And if we can just come to see that right where we are is holy ground – in our jobs and homes, with our co-workers and friends and families. This is where we learn to pray.

In the most natural and simply way possible we learn to pray our experiences by taking up the ordinary events of everyday life and giving them to God. Perhaps we have a crushing failure that gives us more than one sleepless night. Well, we pace the floor with God, telling him of our hurt and our pain and our disappointment. "Why me?" we cry out, "why me?" for frustration and tears and anger are also the language of Simple Prayer. We invite God to walk with us as we grieve the loss of our dream. Maybe an offhand remark by a neighbor triggers a whole explosion of emotions within us: anger, jealousy, fear. Very well, we speak frankly and honestly with God about what are happening and ask him to help us see the hurt behind the emotion.

We should feel peel perfectly free to complain to God, or argue with God, or yell at God. One time the prophet Jeremiah shouted out, "You have seduced me, Yahweh, and I have let myself be seduced; you have overpowered me: you were the stronger. I am a daily laughing – stock, everybody's butt" (Jer. 20:7, JB). And I can well imagine that Jeremiah shook his fist toward heaven as he spoke!

God is perfectly capable of handling our anger and frustration and disappointment. C. S. Lewis counsels us to "lay before Him what is in us, not what ought to be in us."

We must never believe the lie that says that the details of our lives are not the proper content of prayer. For example, we may have been taught that prayer is a sublime and otherworldly activity, that in prayer we are to talk to God about God. As a result, we are inclined to view our experiences as distractions and intrusions into proper prayer. This is an ethereal, decarnate spiritually. We, on the other hand, worship a God who was born in a smelly stable, who walked this earth in blood, sweat, and tears, but who nevertheless lived in perpetual responsiveness to the heavenly Monitor.

And so I urge you: carry on an ongoing conversation with God about the daily stuff of life, a little like Tevye in Fiddler on the Roof.* For now, do not worry about "proper" praying, just talk to God.

"In this manner, therefore, pray." Our Lord gave this as a model prayer after on of His disciples said unto Him, "Lord, teach us to pray, as John also taught his disciples. We are to pray to "Our Father in heaven", because He is all-wise, all-loving, and all-powerful. We are also instructed to pray in the name of Jesus, depending on the meditative influence of the Holy Spirit (Rom. 8:26,27).

> We are to pray for His will to be done in everything.
> We are to pray for the coming of the Kingdom
> We are to pray for our daily necessities.
> We are to pray for forgiveness and are to practice forgiving others.
> We are to pray for the leading of the Lord and for deliverance from evil.
> We are to pray in faith, for "without faith it is impossible to please Him"

CHAPTER 13

DON'T FORGET TO PRAY

But he, being full of the Holy Ghost. Looked up steadfastly into heaven, and saw the glory of God, and Jesus standing on the right hand of God Acts 7:55 Father, during our most trying times, help us to look unto Jesus the Author and Finisher of our faith. O ye gates; even lift them up, ye everlasting doors; and the King of glory shall come in. Who is this King of glory? The Lord of hosts, He is the King of glory. (Psalm 24: 9) All my life I have had a tremendous compassion for hurting and suffering people when other people would put their foot on them. I always tended to have a word of mercy, its praying time.

Perhaps it is because I have had my own pain. I learned to go to the pray room, sometime I would just seat there, I could not pray I just seat thanking God. Perhaps it is because I have had my own pains. When you have suffered, it makes you able to relate to other people's pain. I learned how to put my trust in Jesus Christ, how to have faith and lean on Him. He did not come every time I prayed to Him, he was always on time.

(Matthew 11: 28) Come unto me, all ye that labour and are heavy laden, and I will give you rest. Take my yoke upon you, and learn of me; for I am meek and lowly in heart: and ye shall find rest unto your souls. For my yoke is easy, and my burden is light. Come unto me. Jesus' gracious invitation comes to all "that labour and are heavy laden" with the troubles of life and the sins of their own human nature. By coming to Jesus, becoming His servant, and obeying His direction Jesus will free you from your insurmountable burdens and give you rest, peace, and His Holy Spirit to lead you through life. What trials and cares you carry will be borne with His help and grace.

(Hebrews 4:16) Come Boldly unto the throne. Christ sympathizes with our weaknesses, we can confidently approach the heavenly throne, knowing that our prayers and petitions are welcomed and desired by our heavenly Father. It is called the "throne of grace" because from it flow God's love, help, mercy, forgiveness, spiritual power, the outpouring of the Holy Spirit, His spiritual gifts, the fruit of the Holy Spirit, and all that we need under any circumstances.

Looking back, that was God's way of preparing me for my destiny to preach. Even though I was working faithfully in the vineyard, Even though I was working faithfully it was not what God required of me. I did everything but preach. I just did not want to stand before a crowd of people and preach. I kept running and I kept dreaming. That same stranger in my dream directed me to the scriptures (John 8:15-16) ye judge after the flesh; I judge no man. And yet if I judge, my judgment is true: for I am not alone, but I and the Father that sent me. He said, "Let God be the judge." Jesus judges no man after the flesh.

When we judge we judge after the flesh. Our judgments are limited because we simply do not have all the facts. The Lord Jesus gives the judgment that comes from heaven. God's viewpoints are all that matters. Some time I would go in my pray room just seat there, and other times I would go in and just cried. I was still running and dreaming .The stranger in my dreams told me to read (John 22:17) Jesus saith unto her. Touch me not; for I am not yet ascended to my Father; but go to my brethren, and say unto them, I ascend unto my Father, and your Father; and to my God, and your God.

Jesus gave Mary Magdalene with the task of spreading the good news. The good news of his Glorious resurrection and his ascending back to God. Mary thought she was there to visit Christ's tomb, but Jesus redirected her task and she became the first female evangelist. Mary changed from a fearing, hopeless woman to a faithful, testifying disciple. The difference and change made was the presence of Jesus. She had seen Jesus not the disciples. The disciples went home. She stayed.

Finally, I told my husband about the reoccurring dreams. I told him I had been dreaming the Lord was calling me to preach, He did not question me, he told me if the Lord is calling you to preach I will be with you all the way. But less us go to your pray room and pray about it. We prayed and kept trusting in and believing in God.

I knew this task was not going to be easy. After much consideration, prayers, fasting and trusting in the Lord, I decided to tell my Pastor that the Lord had called me to preach. He said to me, I am with you all the way. "If God be for you, who can be against you? Greater is he that is in you, then he that is in the world.

(1 Corinthians 14:34-35) was truly saying, There was a church meeting a Corinth, in those days, most women were uneducated. The assembling of believers was not for a place for women asking questions. They even prohibited about spiritual matters. Instead, they told them to ask their husbands as home. In understanding Paul's instructions in context, he wants order and harmony in church meetings. Talking to women would be a distraction. Unnecessary talking should not take place in a meeting of the believers that gather to worship God.

Paul was not saying women could not preach, or teach he only called for order in the meeting. Further down in the scriptures, Paul say in (1 Corinthians 14: 37) If any man thinks himself to be a prophet, or spiritual, let him acknowledge that the things that I write unto you are the commandments of the Lord.

Paul removes all ethnic, racial, national social and sexual distinctions with regard to one's spiritual relationship with Jesus Christ. All in Christ are equal heirs of the grace of life. The Promised Spirit and renewal in the image of God. There is neither Jew nor Greek, there is neither bond nor free, there is neither male nor female; for ye are all one in Christ Jesus.

Obeying God's Call Acts 8:31 and he said, How can I, except some man should guide me? And he desired Phillip that he would come up and sit with him. Philip was prompted by the Holy Spirit to go to Gaza, a desert area, where he met a man from another country who needed a clear understanding of who Jesus was. Immediately Philip Obeyed. AS a result of Philip's obedience and witness, the man received Christ as his Savior and was baptized.

Every person is important in God's kingdom. As followers of Christ, we have been given the privilege of sharing the gospel message with those who need a clear understanding of Jesus. Just as Philip's obedience to God made an eternal difference in the life of the Ethiopian eunuch, so can our obedience result in others coming to know and receive Jesus as their Lord and Savior.

THE POWER OF PRAYER

Throughout both the Old and New Testaments we read accounts of how God miraculously intervened in the lives of people who prayed. Today, we serve the same all-powerful God who hears and answers the prayers of His people. When Peter was arrested for preaching the gospel, he was put in prison and chained to prison guards. Fellow believers immediately assembled to pray unceasingly for Peter's release. God answered their prayers, and through a mighty act of divine deliverance, Peter walked out of prison a free man. Psalm 4:3 But know that the LORD hath set apart him that is godly for himself: the LORD will hear when I call unto him.

The godly are those who are faithful and devoted to God. David knew that God would hear him when he called and would answer him. We, too, can be confident that God listens and answers when we call on him. Sometimes we think God will not here us because we have fallen short of his high standards for holy living. But God has forgiven us and he will listen to us. When you feel that your prayers are "bouncing off the ceiling," remember that as a believer you have been set apart by God and that he loves you. He hears and answers (although his answers may not be what you expect). Look at your problems in the light of God's power instead of looking at God in the shadow of your problems.

The secret of a close relationship with God is to pray to him earnestly in the morning. In the morning, our minds are freer from problems, and then we can commit the whole day to God. Sometimes we think God will not hear us because we have fallen short of his high standards for holy living.

But God has forgiven us and he will listen to us. When you feel that your prayers are "bouncing off the ceiling." Remember that as a believer you have been set apart by God and that he loves you. He hears and answers (although his answers may not be what you expect). Look at your problems in the light of God's power instead of looking at God in the shadow of your problems. Praying for relief from despair. We must continue to trust God even when he doesn't answer us immediately. Solomon blessed the Lord and prayed for the people. His prayer can be a pattern for our prayers. He had five basic requests: (1) for God's presence: (2)for the desire to do God's will in everything (3) for the desire and ability to obey God's laws and commandments (4) for help with daily needs (5) for the spread of God's Kingdom to the entire world. These prayer requests are just as applicable today as in Solomon's time.

PRAYING FOR RESULTS

Regardless of any man's ability, he will fail if his endeavors are not backed by prayer. The major cause of failure in Christian enterprises is an omission of prayer. Whether your goal is to witness to one man or to preach the gospel to nations, you will succeed or fail based entirely on your prayer life. One percent of your time spent in prayer will produce only 1 percent results. Eighty percent prayer will bring 80 percent results. This formula works every time. The obvious question is, "But how can I expect to receive 100 percent results? I can't spend all of my time in prayer." Oh yes, you can!

Prayer is an attitude. It involves more than just making requests. Prayer is communicating with God. You can live in an attitude of prayer constantly, being in communion and fellowship with your heavenly Father every hour of the day.

In order to get results in prayer, you must be convinced of one basic fact: **God wants to answer your prayers.** In fact, He is as ready and willing to answer you as He was to answer Jesus during His early ministry. This may be difficult for you to believe, but it is true.

I remember how amazed I was to learn about God's willingness to answer my prayers. I had always though of myself as unworthy. I thought, **why would God bother to answer my prayers?** Ignorance of God's Word kept me from receiving His best in my life.

Once I realized the importance of the Word of God, my attitude changed. I realized that God does not see His children as unworthy. Notice how Jesus prayed: "**...that the world may know that thou hast sent me, and hast loved them, as thou hast loved me**" (John 17:23). Just think! God loves you and me as much as he loves Jesus! **We are worthy!**

Knowing that God is ready to answer your prayers will make you serious about your prayer life. Never take your prayer privilege lightly. Because you are a child of God, you have an open invitation from Him to come into the throne room any time you wish. You do not have to enter His presence crawling on your hands and knees. You can boldly stand before God without a sense of guilt or shame or condemnation.

> *"Let us therefore come boldly unto the throne of grace, that we may obtain mercy, and find grace to help in time of need"*
> (Hebrews 4:16).

To understand what pray is, it help to realize what it is not. Prayer is not an emotional release. It is not an escape valve. It is much more than just asking God for a favor. Perhaps most important of all, prayer is not a religious exercise.

You should be praying for results every time you pray. Do not just speak empty words. Jesus said in Matthew 6:7 *"But when ye pray, use not vain repetitions, as the heathen do: for they think that they shall be heard for their much speaking."*

The beauty of your prayer does not get the ear of God. He responds to faith. To explain, let me give you an example from my own experience. Not long after I became a Christian, I asked a minister to pray for me. I was expecting to hear a long, beautiful prayer –one that would cause people to fall on their knees in repentance before God! What I heard was just the opposite. He laid her hand on my chest, bowed his head, and said, "Lord, bless her. Meet his every need." He then turned and walked away. I was left standing there thinking, *how could he do that to me? I have big problems. It should have taken at least 20 minutes of hard praying to cover everything.*

One major difference separated that minister and me: the degree of faith at work in our lives. He was operating in faith, praying exactly what he meant. I was a baby Christian, looking for a physical manifestation of some kind. It makes no difference how long you pray or how beautiful your words. **Praying in faith is merely having confidence in God's willingness to use His power to answer your prayer.**

The man who knows the importance of prayer is very difficult to defeat. He knows that, regardless of what comes, he can pray and God will move in his behalf.

The key to success in prayer is expecting results. Many Christians think, I'll *pray and maybe something will happen.* They say, "I'm just hoping and praying."

If you are hoping to get results, you will never receive from God. "Hoping to get" is not the same as "believing you receive." The promises of God bring you hope in hopeless situations. However, hope has no substance in itself. "I hope to get healed someday." You hope to receive someday, but someday never come. **Faith brings hope into reality and gives substance to it.** Hebrews 11:1 says: *"Now faith is the substance of things hoped for, the evidence of things not seen."* The object of hope becomes a reality through faith. Hope is always in the future. Faith is always now.

The number one rule in praying for results is: base your prayer on God's Word. It can be relied on just as you would depend on the word of your best friend. If you trust him, you will believe what he says. Faith in God operates the same way. **God's Word is the integrity of God Himself** (John 17:17).

As an example, let's use the prayer for salvation. Your first step is to go to the Word and find out what God says you must do to be saved. Romans 10:9-10, *"That if thou shalt confess with thy mouth the Lord Jesus, and shalt believe in thine heart that God hath raised him from the dead, thou shalt be saved. For with the heart man believeth unto righteousness; and with the mouth confession is made unto salvation."*

This scripture is the basis for your prayer. You confess with your mouth Jesus as Lord and you believe in your heart that God has raised Him from the dead; God's Word says it so you can accept it as fact. When you fulfill these two prerequisites, the Word says, *"Thou shalt be saved."* You must receive it by faith.

When you pray the prayer of salvation, you may not feel differently. Realize that your feelings do not have anything to do with it. **God's Word is His part of your prayer life.** He has already said in His Word, *"Thou shalt be saved."* You have allowed the Word of God to engineer your prayer. It makes no difference how you feel. Exercise your faith. By the authority of God's Word you are saved! In Mark 11:24 Jesus said, *"What things so ever ye desire, when ye pray, believe that ye receive them, and ye shall have them."*

God's Word is His will. When you pray in line with the Word, you have automatically prayed in line with God's will. 1 John 5:14-15 says, *"And this is the confidence that we have in him, that, if we ask any thing according to his will, he heareth us: And if we know that he hear us, whatsoever we ask, we know that we have the petitions that we desired of him."* Your prayer for salvation, based on God's Word, was clearly heard by the Father. After you pray and receive your salvation by faith, you then simply thank God for it.

Second Corinthians 5:17 says, *". . . if any man be in Christ, he is a new creature: old things are passed away; behold, all things are become new."* See yourself as a new creation. Visualize that the man you once were died the death of the Cross and was raised to new life by the power of the Holy Spirit (Romans 6:4). This is actually what happened. You prayed according to the Word of God, therefore you are saved.

Praying for healing involves the same faith principles. Search God's Word for your answer. Isaiah 53:5 says, *"But he was wounded for our transgressions, he was bruised for our iniquities: the chastisement of our peace was upon him; and with his stripes we are healed."* Matthew 8:17 says, *"Himself took our infirmities, and bare our sicknesses."*

Undoubtedly healing is God's will. According to these scriptures, Jesus paid the price – not only for sin, but for sickness, disease and the consequences of sin. More religious traditions have discounted God's will for healing than those that discredit salvation. To know God's will toward healing, look at Jesus. Jesus said, *"...he that seen me hath seen the Father"* (John 14:9). During His time on earth, Jesus was the express image of God (Hebrews 1:3). What did He do? He healed the sick. Acts 10:38 says, *"...God anointed Jesus of Nazareth with the Holy Ghost and power: who went about doing good, and healing all that were oppressed of the devil; for God was with him."*

The prayer for healing is a simple one. You say, "Father, in the Name of Jesus, I see in Your Word that healing belongs to me. I believe I receive it. I thank you for it. I act upon it now." Once you have prayed, TRUST. Do not let Satan convince you that you are still sick. He will try his best to sell his lies. **Stand your ground!** Say, "Satan, it is written...." Then begin to speak what God's Word says about your healing. Just as he fled at the command of Jesus' words, Satan will have to flee when you speak God's Word in faith (Matthew 4:1-11). He has no defense against the Word of God when it is spoken in faith by a believer.

When you begin your prayer based on God's Word, you are starting with the answer. The Word contains the answer to every problem that could confront you.

The next step in praying effectively is found in Mark 11:24. Jesus said, *"What things so ever ye desire, when ye pray, believe that ye receive them, and ye shall have them."* This places a qualification on your prayer. You have to believe you receive when you pray. Do not wait until the manifestation comes to believe you receive.

This will seem very difficult at first. But as you get to know God personally, you will become convinced that His Word is true. The problem area will diminish. **Make a quality decision to believe God's Word.** Numbers 23:19 says: *"God is not a man, that he should lie; neither the son of man, that he should repent: hath he said, and shall he not do it? Or hath he spoken, and shall he not make it good?"* You can trust His integrity. When you pray, all you have to do is apply your faith.

Where does faith come from? How do you get faith? Faith come by hearing and hearing by the Word of God (Romans 10:17). Every believer is dealt the measure of faith (Romans 12:3). He must develop that faith by spending time in the Word of God. The application of your faith in any given situation is directly related to your knowledge of God. You could not have faith to be saved before you knew it was God's will to save you. If you feel that you need more faith, realize that you already have faith. What you need is more personal knowledge of God through time in the Word.

Once you have prayed in faith, hold fast to your confession. God is aware of your situation. His power went to work the instant you prayed in faith. You can rest assured that what you prayed will come to pass. *Maintain* your faith by keeping your confession in line with the Word.

> **There remained therefore a rest to the**
>
> **People of God. For he that is entered into his**
>
> **Rest, he also hath ceased from his own works,**
>
> **As God did from him. Let us labour therefore**
>
> **To enter into that rest, lest any man fall after**
>
> **The same example of unbelief. For the word**

> **Of God is quick, and powerful, and sharper**
>
> **Than any two-edged sword, piercing even to**
>
> **The dividing asunder of soul and spirit, and**
>
> **Of the joints and marrow, and is a discerner**
>
> **Of the thoughts and intents of the heart. Nei-**
>
> **ther is there any creature that is not manifest**
>
> **in his sight: but all things are naked and**
>
> **Opened unto the eyes of him with whom we**
>
> **have to do. Seeing then that we have a great**
>
> **high priest, that is passed into the heavens,**
>
> **Jesus the Son of God, let us hold fast our pro-**
>
> **fession (Hebrews 4:9-14).**

Speak only words that agree with what you desire. Jesus is seated at the right hand of the Father. As your High Priest, he is seeing to it that the whole system works the way God said it would!

The importance of speaking the right words cannot be measured. Faith is released with the mouth. Words are the vehicles. God spoke faith-filled words when He created the universe. Hebrews 11:3 says, *"Through faith we understand that the worlds were framed by the word of God. . . ."* God spoke and the Spirit of God used the faith in those words to create the worlds.

Even Jesus ministered during His earthly ministry by speaking words. At the tomb of Lazarus, He said, *"Lazarus, come forth,"* and he did (John 11:43). At the city of Nain, Jesus stopped a funeral procession and said, *"My son, I say unto thee, arise."* The boy was raised from the dead. Matthew 8:16 says that Jesus cast out the devil with His Word. According to Psalm 107:20, God sent His Word and it healed the children of Israel.

When faith words are spoken, they must be backed by corresponding actions. James 2:17, *The Amplified Bible says, "So also faith if it does not have the works (deeds and actions of obedience to back it up), by itself is destitute of power – inoperative, dead."* God's Word instructs us to be doers and not hearers only. In applying faith, two elements are involved: words and actions. **Real Bible faith demands action.**

You have to act by faith, not according to your feelings or reasoning's. Faith is based on eternal truth and is more dependable then the evidence of your physical senses. According to 2 Corinthians 4:18, we are not to look at the things which are seen, but at things which are not seen. The things which are visible are temporal, or changeable. The things which are invisible are eternal; they never change. Don't focus your attention on what you perceive through your five physical senses. Keep your heart fixed on the Word of God. Then what you see will come in line with the Word.

To believe God's Word rather than physical circumstances is to talk and act the answer instead of the problem. **Acting on the Word puts faith into motion.** You cannot expect results from your prayer without the operation of faith.

One incident that occurred during the ministry of Jesus is a fine example of faith in action. Jesus was teaching in a private home. The crowd was so large there was no room for anyone else. Some men had brought a sick friend to Jesus to be healed. When they could not reach Him because of the throng of people, they refused to be denied.

They knocked a hole in the roof and lowered him into the room on a stretcher.

The owner of that house thought as much of his roof as you think of yours. How do you suppose he reacted when they tore a hole in his roof? These men had one thing in mind: to reach Jesus. They put aside their own dignity and refused to fear the owner of the house or the people around them. When they lowered the sick man into the room, Luke 5:20 says that Jesus **SAW their faith.** The invisible force of faith because visible through their action! In response to faith, Jesus forgave the man's sins and healed his body.

What Jesus did 2,000 years ago, He will do today. He is the same yesterday, today and forever (Hebrews 13:8).

Once you have prayed, hold fast to your confession. Refuse to speak contrary to the Word of God. Do not allow circumstances to sway you. Act as though it were already done.

When you apply your faith accurately according to God's Word, you will get results. You will experience Hebrews 4:16 for yourself. *"Let us therefore come boldly unto the throne of grace, that we may obtain mercy, and find grace to help in time of need."* It does not say "Come and hope to get." It says, "Come **obtain!**"

A very misunderstood concept throughout the religious world is that it is extremely difficult to get God to answer prayer at all – much less answer all prayer. That is a lie of Satan and absolutely contrary to the Word of God. **When you believe God's Word in your heart and you pray in line with His Word you have every right to expect your prayer to bring results.** Jesus said: *"Verily I say unto you, If ye have faith, and doubt not, ye shall not only do this which is done to the fig tree, but also if ye shall say unto this mountain, Be thou removed, and be thou cast into the sea; it shall be done. And all things, whatsoever ye shall ask in prayer, believing, ye shall receive"* (Matthew 21:21-22).

If God will answer the prayer of a sinner to be saved, He will certainly answer the prayers of born-again believers who come to Him in faith concerning their lives.

Satan uses doubt with great skill and cunning to cause you to fail. He knows the importance of getting you to waver. He constantly tries to throw doubt and unbelief into your consciousness. If you begin to wonder whether you have the answer, Satan will purpose to secure a foothold in your mind, making you faith ineffective. This will cause you to be defeated.

Matthew 14:24-31 is a perfect illustration. Jesus' disciples were traveling to the other side of the sea by ship.

> **But the ship was now in the midst of the sea,**
>
> **Tossed with waves: for the wind was contrary.**
>
> **And in the fourth watch of the night Jesus**
>
> **Went unto them, walking on the sea. And**
>
> **When the disciples saw him walking on the**
>
> **Sea, they were troubled, saying, It is a sprit;**
>
> **And they cried out for fear. But straightway**
>
> **Jesus spake unto them, saying, Be of good**
>
> **Cheer; it is I; be not afraid. And Peter**
>
> **Answered him and said, Lord if it be thou,**
>
> **Bid me come unto thee on the water. And**

He said, Come. And when Peter was come down out of the ship, he walked on the water, to go to Jesus. But when he saw the wind boisterous, he was afraid; and beginning to sink, he cried, saying, Lord, save me. And immediately Jesus stretched forth his Hand, and caught him, and said unto him O thou of little faith, wherefore did thou doubt?

When Peter cried out to Jesus, He answered him with one word: "Come." That command carried the authority necessary to defy all natural power. Faith supported him on the water. Peter stepped out of the boat into a supernatural experience. When he *swathe* wind, however, he became *afraid* and failed. **He saw, he feared, and he sank!**

Three elements are always involved in defeat: **SEE + FEAR + DOUBT = DEFEATED FAITH**

Doubt was the thief that robbed Peter of God's best. Great sermons have been made about how Jesus was there to save him. God's best was not that he be rescued in the nick of time before he was overwhelmed by a raging sea! Peter had an opportunity to walk in the supernatural in spite of what was happening in the natural. *Faith or Fear* – you cannot be functioning in both at the same time. Doubt causes defeat!

In praying effectively, a vital part of your success is knowing how to refuse doubt, fear, and unbelief. If you are concentrating on your circumstances instead of the Word, you are building an inner image of the problem and not the solution. What you see on the inside will determine your attitude. If all your envision are your negative circumstances, you will doubt God's Word. Satan will take advantage of you to thwart your faith process.

Doubt operates in the mental realm. God's Word operates in the spiritual realm. Our responsibility is to use the spiritual weapons at our disposal. *"For though we walk in the flesh, we do not war after the flesh: (For the weapons of our warfare are not carnal, but mighty through God to the pulling down of strong holds;) Casting down imaginations, and every high thing that exalteth itself against the knowledge of God, and bringing into captivity every thought to the obedience of Christ."* (2 Corinthians 10:3-5). Peter's battle was not with natural forces. The combat was spiritual. Natural law was subject to the power inherent in Jesus' word, come. By stepping out of the boat, Peter acted on the authority in that word. We can walk in the supernatural in spite of life's storms raging against us. Our spiritual weapons are *mighty!*

Maintain control of your mind. Do not allow doubt or fear to enter your consciousness. Be ready to refuse any thought or imagination contrary to your prayer. When doubt comes, refuse to give it any place. Be selective about the thoughts you entertain. Do not build inner images of defeat! Control your thought life according to Philippians 4:6-9. Learn to think on things that are true, honest, just, pure, lovely, and of good report.

Satan uses doubt and fear to bluff you into accepting defeat. You can overcome him by the power of God and faith in His Word.

You can avoid failure by *preparing* to succeed. Once you have prayed in faith, you must **stand your ground until the manifestation comes.** Fight the good fight of faith. Stand firm on the Word and believe God for results. Give Him the opportunity to do something with your circumstances. God is on *your* side! Prepare to succeed, not to fail. **When you pray in Jesus' Name, according to the Word in Faith, God will quickly respond to you (John 16:23).**

Suppose you prayed for healing. Then you think, *What will I do if God doesn't heal me? Maybe I had better get an appointment with the doctor. He's awfully busy this time of year. I might not be able to see him. Then if God doesn't heal me, I'll be in a mess!*

With that attitude, believing God will be a waste of time. The person who thinks that way will be unable to receive from God. Before he prays, he is already preparing to fail. He is double minded and, according to James 1:8, unstable in all his ways. The man who wavers in his mind will never receive from God. He is like a wave of the sea, driven with the wind and tossed about in every direction. He has a backup plan "just in case." The moment he feels the least bit sick, he will operate in fear and unbelief. When he feels well, he will act in faith, but he will never achieve any concrete results.

If the though, *But what am I going to do if I fail?* Comes, don't give place to it. If you have a setback, just get back on the Word of God. The power of God is the same whether you feel like it or not. Receive the Word into your heart. Renew your mental attitude to the Word. Prepare to succeed and you will receive the manifestation in the physical realm.

You may ask, "But how do I prepare to succeed?" Keep your attention on God's Word. Look at Proverbs 4:20-22: *"My son, attend to my words; incline thine ear unto my sayings. Let them not depart from thine eyes; keep them in the midst of thine heart. For they are life unto those that find them, and health to all their flesh."*

Do not listen to the voice of circumstances around you. Keep the Word of God before you. Do whatever is necessary to keep Satan and circumstances under control. If that means reading the Word 200 times a day, then do it.

Jesus said in Matthew 6:22, *"The light of the body is the eye: if therefore thine eye be single, thy whole body shall be full of light."* Your body responds to what it is fed through the eyes. If you are believing God for healing, you must feed your consciousness with the Word of God which will bring healing. Waste no time on useless activities. Be diligent to spend your time in God's Word. **The Word of God will set you free. Make plans to succeed!**

Together, these principles will bring the desired results: the manifestation of answered prayer by God's supernatural power. At that moment, you have a realization of God's ability from your own personal experience, not just through another's testimony. This is probably the most exciting thing that could happen. You realize God moved because *you* prayed and used your faith.

Why don't we just take God's Word for what it says? For example, in Mark 11:23,24, Jesus gave us a pattern for biblical confession and prayer. This is one way you possess all that God has for you as a believer. These scriptures show us *the God-kind of faith.*

Why do many believers have problems possessing all the promises of God for their lives? Is it that they don't *believe?* Well, usually it's that they don't *confess* God's Word before they see the answer.

In Mark 11:23,24, Jesus explained God's inevitable law of faith – the God-kind of faith. God's law of faith is to believe in your heart that you receive your petition when you pray. Then you *confess* with your mouth that your need is met according to God's Word. That's how you *receive* your answer by faith.

And Jesus answering saith unto them, have faith in God [have the God-kind of faith].

For verily I say unto you, That whosoever shall SAY unto this mountain, Be thou removed, and be thou cast into the sea; and shall not doubt in his heart, but shall BELIEVE that those things which he SAITH shall come to pass; he shall have whatsoever he SAITH.

Therefore I say unto you, What things so ever ye desire, WHEN YE PRAY, BELIEVE THAT YE receive them, and ye shall have them.

Mark 11:22-24

Jesus introduces Mark 11:23,24 by saying, "Have faith in God." In the margin of my Bible it says, "Have the faith of God." Other translations read, "Have the faith that God gives," or "Have the God-kind of faith."

Then in verse 23, Jesus begins to explain the God-kind of faith. The God-kind of faith has to do with what you say or confess. The word "say" is used in some form three times in Mark 11:23: say, *saith*, and *saith*. So what you say is important if you want faith that works.

Evidently, Jesus was telling us that we're going to have more trouble with our saying than we are with our *believing*. That's one reason why it's scriptural to continue to speak the Word of God about a situation.

Many people read this passage of Scripture and say, "Well, it was Jesus doing the talking, all right. But I don't believe He meant what He said."

If Jesus didn't mean what He said – that we can have what we say – then why didn't He say what He meant? No, we don't have to try to figure out and interpret what Jesus said! In this passage of Scripture, Jesus explains to us how the God-kind of faith works.

I want you to notice that there are three important points in Mark 11:23,24. First, Jesus said that the one who practices the God-kind of faith must *not doubt* in his heart.

Second, Jesus said that a person must *believe* that those things he says will come to pass. Third, when he *believes* God's Word in his heart and *confesses* it with his mouth, then he shall have whatsoever he says.

If what you say with your mouth is a result of what you believe in your heart, and it's based on God's Word, then the Word will work for you. That's how you activate the God-kind of faith or the faith that comes from God.

The God-kind of faith is how you receive everything God has promised you in His Word. Believe God's promise, *Confess* God's promise, and *receive* God's promise.

You see, there are a lot Scriptures in the Word of God. Many of them tell us what Christ has ready done for us, so since Jesus has already bought and paid for our inheritance at the Cross of Calvary, then it's ours now. Think about it! We don't have to wait until we get to heaven. The promises of God are ours now! They belong to us.

The climax of Mark 11:23 comes when Jesus said, "You shall have whatever you say." Of course, what you say has to be based on the promises in God's Word. If you're going to run around just claming anything, you're going to get into trouble.

So when the Bible says you can have what you say, it's not talking about just anything you say. It has to be something that's promised to you in God's Word. If the Bible says something belongs to you, then you need to talk in line with God's Word, not against it, so you can receive your inheritance in Christ – your promised land.

Some believes have acted on what they thought was "faith" and made all kinds of confessions that weren't bases in the Word, and it was nothing but presumption and foolishness.

Preparing To Pray

May the words of my mouth and the meditation of my heart be pleasing in your sight, O Lord, my Rock and my Redeemer.

Psalm 19:14

A study of the meditative lifestyles of some believers reveals the ample time they set aside to live close to God and to listen to Him. John Wesley, the British founder of Methodism, described how he was able to achieve this: "Though I am always in haste, I am never in a hurry because I never undertake more work than I can go through with calmness of spirit."

To develop a lifestyle of prayer in our lives, we need to have that same calmness of spirit. To achieve that, we must first prepare our hearts and minds for prayer. We wouldn't think of going on a long car trip without checking the map to see where we're going, packing what we'll need, and making sure our car is in working condition and has a full tank of gas.

In the same way, we need to prepare ourselves for prayer. Our road map is God's Word. We should study it to know God's promises and direction for our life. We should have no excess baggage on our trip, which means we need to clear away any distractions so we can focus fully on aligning ourselves with our Redeemer in prayer. And to make sure we're in working condition, we need to clean our thoughts, have the right attitude for prayer and have the right relationship with God and others.

PRAY AND TIME

Do not let this Book of the Law depart from your mouth; meditate on it day and night, so that you may be careful to do everything written in it. Then you will be prosperous and successful.
Joshua 1:8

The Word of God must permeate every aspect of our lives in order for us to be able to pray. And God commands us, along with Joshua, to learn His Word and speak it in prayer to receive His blessings. Be learning His Word, we learn about our Creator and Redeemer. We know His will for us, His expectations for us, and His love and grace. We see Him more clearly, and we align our thoughts and wishes with His.

God wants us to know Him in a personal relationship built through prayer. He doesn't want us to just do good works or contribute time or money. If we do those things without a close relationship with our Redeemer, we're not doing His will. God knows the desires of our heart, and His wants us to hunger after His presence.

Reading God's Word as part of any time we've set aside to pray also helps focus that time on God, not on ourselves or worldly distractions. When we study His Word, we put God as our top priority and we want to be united with Him through prayer.

Be still before the Lord and wait patiently for him.
Psalm 37:7

When we're in prayer with God, we need to be focused solely on Him – to "be still" as the psalmist says, seeking to hear His voice in our life. As we develop our lifestyle of prayer, we strive to focus our thoughts on our Redeemer all the time. (We'll talk later about building this kind of relationship). To stay focused, we need to deal with the distractions that are bound to crop up and could affect our relationship with God.

On way is to set aside special times during our day that we commit solely to prayer. When we do that, we can schedule other tasks and appointments around that time. We can unplug the phone and not answer the door. We give that time to God alone. A time of solitude allows us to bring our whole being to the Lord and empty ourselves mentally to seek Him.

> *What is true, whatever is noble, whatever is right, whatever is pure, whatever is lovely, whatever is admirable – If anything is excellent or praiseworthy – think about such things.*
>
> *Philippians 4:8*

Before we pray, we need to clean our thoughts. We should take time to wash away every thought of the world and its agendas and let our minds be at rest. We can't be focusing our thoughts on Him when we're worried about problems at work or at home. We should be bringing our cares and concerns to God in prayer – not letting them keep us from Him. For if we allow those issues to clutter our minds, we won't be able to seek His will and listen for His guidance.

Then, once we've handed those concerns to the Lord, we need to fill our minds with the Holy Spirit. We should have the beauty of a clean mind that can think well for the Lord.

> *To some who were confident of their own righteousness and looked down on everybody else, Jesus told this parable: "Two men went up to the temple to pray, one a Pharisee and the other a tax collector. The Pharisee stood up and prayed about himself: 'God, I thank you that I am not like other men – robbers, evildoers, adulterers – or even like this tax collector. I fast twice a week and give a tenth of all I get.' But the tax collector stood at a distance. He would not even look up to heaven, but beat his breast and said, 'God, have mercy on me, a sinner.' I tell you that this man,*

> *rather than the other, went home justified before God. For everyone who exalts himself will be humbled, and he who humbles himself will be exalted."*
>
> Luke 18:9-14

In prayer, as in everything, our motives are very important. If we ask for things to please ourselves or impress others, we have the wrong motives. If we're after what we can get for ourselves, rather than being surrendered to God and His will, our prayers are not proper. As James 4:3 says, "When you ask, you do not receive, because you ask with wrong motives that you may spend what you get on your pleasures."

Often we really want God to be something He is not. There is a God we want and a God who is, and they are not the same. Many times we don't understand God. As Isaiah 55:8 says, "For my thoughts are not your thoughts, neither are your ways my ways, declares the Lord." It is through prayer that we begin to bridge the gap, to get a glimpse of who God is and who He wants us to be.

Therefore, in our prayer lives, we need a proper gaze, focused on Jesus Christ. If we allow our gaze to be on our requests, those requests will consume us. We end up telling God what we need to be done; we attempt to control Him.

But the Lord is not a servant or an errand boy responding to our wishes. If He gave us everything we ask for – to live longer, to get rid of nearsightedness, to own a bigger house – we'd be satisfied with this world and we wouldn't look forward to being with Him in heaven. The reason for our salvation is not to be saved from our problems but to be saved from our selfishness. Selfishness is more than behavior. When we're selfish, we focus on our own wants and needs. When we're selfless, we're inclined to God. It's the selfish who demand, and they're miserable. It's the selfless who give, and they become close to Christ. The selfish keep wondering what the selfless are talking about, for they never understand.

As we said earlier, one of the reasons we pray is to receive from God. He wants to provide for us, but He also wants our thoughts and motives in line with His will.

So we pray to God Almighty as our Redeemer and Savior, seeking His will in our lives and having faith that He will provide for our every need. Psalm 37:4 assures us of this ; Delight yourself in the Lord and he will give you the desires of your heart."

If our prayers were answered for the wrong reasons, we would continue to come to God for what we get from Him. We would continue to pray so we could gain material goods. Our selfishness would be fed, and we wouldn't recognize that we should surrender our will to God.

When we ask of God, we should as in His name for His will to be done. Jesus tells us in John 16:23-24, "I tell you the truth, my Father will give you whatever you ask in my name. Until now you have not asked for anything in my name. Ask and you will receive, and your joy will be complete."

When we do that, we hand Him our selfishness, our desire for control, our desire for worldly possessions. We have a feeling of love that is a result of God redeeming us from our sins.

Does prayer change events? It may. But the most important effect of prayer is that it changes the person who is praying to become more like the One to whom he is praying – our Redeemer.

> *Dear friends, if our hearts do not condemn us, we have confidence before God and receive from him anything we ask, because we obey his commands and do what pleases him.*
>
> *1 John 3:21-22*

> *But your iniquities have separated you from your God;*
> *your sins have hidden his face from you, so that he will*
> *not hear.*
>
> Isaiah 59:2

In the same way that we clean our thoughts and make sure we have the right motives in prayer, we also must clean our hearts of sin against our Lord. If we try to pray, but try to hide sin from Him, we create a wall that prayer cannot overcome.

We must be prepared to be honest with God, to confess our sins and our weakness. He knows them already. But in being honest with our Lord, we seek reunion with Him and can be made whole with Him again. Psalm 66:18-19 says, "If I had cherished sin in my heart, the Lord would not have listened; but God has surely listened and heard my voice in prayer."

We must clear away any stumbling blocks that would isolate us from Him and be prepared to ask, and receive, His forgiveness for our sins.

> *Anyone who claims to be in the light, but hates his brother*
> *is still in the darkness.*
>
> 1 John 2:9

In the same way that we reconcile our relationship with God, we must reconcile our relationships with others. And just as God forgives our sins, so we must forgive others. Mark 11:25 says, "And when you stand praying, if you hold anything against anyone, forgive him, so that your Father in heaven may forgive you your sins."

The greatest part of prayer is to forgive others. Righteousness, which is the ultimate aspect of the Christian walk, is impossible to achieve until we have been forgiven and in turn forgive. Unless we forgive, we can never be in a true relationship with the Lord and be able to do the things He would have us do.

To prepare ourselves for prayer we must be ready to listen to our Redeemer. It takes time, effort and practice to put the distractions of the world – work, hectic schedules, families – on hold so we can study His Word and seek Him.

We also must always put ourselves on the line to have an open, honest and joyous relationship with God in prayer. We have to be vigilant in making sure our motives are aligned with God's motives. And we must be honest with Him about the sins that keep us from being inclined to Him. In the same way, we must have open relationships with others. It can be hard work, but the benefits far out weight the risks.

> *Therefore we do not lose heart. Though outwardly we are wasting away. Yet inwardly we are being renewed day by day. For our light and momentary troubles are achieving for us an eternal glory that far outweighs them all. So we fix our eyes not on what is seen, but on what is unseen. For what is seen is temporary, but what is unseen is eternal.*
> *II Corinthians 4:16-18*

"Men always ought to pray." Prayer is imperative. You are commanded to pray. Because prayer is the only way to get things from God. "You do not have because you do not ask" James 4:2. There is joy un prayer John 16:24. Prayer will save you out of all your troubles Ps. 34:6 OT. Prayer can unlock the treasure chest of God's wisdom James 1:5. Prayer is a channel of power Jer 33:3 OT. Sinners can be saved when they pray in faith Rom. 10:13, 14.

It is a rare privilege to pray; because it brings you into close fellowship with God, admitting your need for Him and your utter dependence upon Him.

The Bible is filled with answered prayers from Genesis to Revelation. You are commanded to pray, and God has promised to answer (Jer. 33:3 OT).

> *"If you abide in Me, and My words abide in you, you will ask what you desire, and it shall be done for you (John 15:7).*

In this Scripture, there are two requirements for answers to prayer. First, you are to abide in Him; that is, to continue in Him. It means to remain in His perfect will at all cost (Rom 12:1, 2). Second, His words are to abide in you; they are to become a vital part of your life. You are to be filled with and guided by His words (Col. 3:16, 17). Meet these two requirements, and your prayers will be answered.

The answer is sometimes immediate. Peter walked on the water to go to Jesus, and as he began to sink, he prayed, "Lord, save me!" The answer was immediate. The answer is sometimes delayed. The delay is according to His will (Rom. 8:28). The resurrection of Lazarus is a good example of delayed answer to prayer. Lazarus was sick. Mary and Martha sent for Jesus to come and heal him. But Jesus delayed coming until Lazarus was dead and in the tomb for four days. Then He came and raised Lazarus from the dead. The answer was delayed – but not denied (John 11:1-44). The answer is sometimes "no." When God answers with a "no," He always accompanies the answer with peace and grace (Phil. 4:6, 7) (2Cor. 12:7-10).

The answer is sometimes different from what you expect. You pray for perseverance and God sends tribulation – because "tribulation produces perseverance" (Rom. 5:3). God answers all your prayers – not according to your wishes, but according to His perfect will.

The Battlefield of Prayer

Every believer is involved in spiritual warfare. The problems we face are brought about by satanic forces – principalities, powers, rulers of darkness of this world and wicked spirits in heavenly places. Our responsibility is to use the weapons of our warfare to fight the good fight of faith. What are those weapons? The Name of Jesus, the Word of God, the Holy Spirit and the gifts of the Spirit.

Prayer is the battlefield. The time spent in prayer is the base of supply. The armor described in Ephesians 6 is prayer armor. It serves one vital purpose: to combat Satan and win!

Your enemy is not other people. Satan is the source of all your trouble. Some people believe that God sends tribulation and trials. But God has provided the weapons and armor that get us out of trouble! Satan is the troublemaker! Not God! Not your neighbor! Not your co-worker!

In combat a good strategist knows the importance of cutting the enemy's supply and dividing his troop. Defeat is inevitable. Without a supply of food, water and ammunition, it will be only a matter of time until the enemy is in his hands. In fact, all he has to do is sit back and wait. If we are not spending time in prayer actively combating Satan, then he can easily overtake us.

Satan's strategy is to move in and cut off our supply. Much of our failure in the past has been Satan's success in dividing the Church. Bit thank God, the Body of Christ is coming together throughout the earth. People of all denominational back-grounds are uniting in the power of the Holy Spirit. Believers are discovering more and more each day the power of God that is available to them. They are putting on their prayer armor, preparing to do battle in the world of the spirit. The barriers of denominations are crumbling like the walls of Jericho!

Thank God, we have authority over Satan and his cohorts. We are to be strong in the Lord and in the power of His might. We must master our weapons and use them effectively. If we expect to win the war, we must spend the time to reinforce our troops through prayer.

As a believer, you are a soldier in the army of God. Visualize yourself standing ready for the battle with the armor of God protecting you – your lions girt with the truth. The breastplate of righteousness is in place. Your feet are shod with the preparation of the gospel of peace. ABOVE ALL, you are holding the shield of faith to quench ALL the fiery darts of the wicked. You have the helmet of salvation on your head and the sword of the Spirit – the Word of God – in your hand.

The shield of faith is a vital part of the Christian's armor. You are to put on the "whole armor of God", because the Christian life is a warfare, a spiritual conflict. As Paul names the different parts of the Christian' s armor, he comes to the shield and emphasizes its importance by saying, "Above all, taking the shield of faith. . . ." (Ephesians 6:16).

For with the shield of faith, nothing can hurt you; ". . . in all these things we are more than conquerors through Him who loved us" (Rom. 8:37).

The importance of faith is seen in that: You cannot be saved without faith (John 3:36). You cannot live victoriously over the world without faith (1 John 5:4). You cannot please God with faith (Heb. 11:6). You cannot pray without faith (James 1:6). You cannot have peace with God without faith (Rom. 5:1). You cannot have joy without faith (1 Pet 1:8). You are justified by faith and not by works (Gal. 2:16). You are to live by faith (Gal. 2:20). Christ dwells in your heart by faith (Eph. 3:17). The Holy Spirit is received by faith (Gal 3:2). "Whatever is not from faith is sin" (Rom. 14:23). Faith is important because it honors God, and God always honors faith.

Faith defies reason; it moves mountains (Matt. 17:14-21). Faith does not always face facts; it never gives up (Heb.11:32-39). Faith says, "God is working out His perfect will in my life, and I can wait, endure, and suffer." Faith does not make anything easy, but it does make all things possible.

You are covered head to foot with the powerful armor of God. It is strong and will withstand any onslaught of the enemy. Let me show you how it works.

"And having done all, to stand. Stand therefore, having your lions girt about with truth." When Satan tells you in your mind that you will never see the manifestation of your prayers, that is the time to gird yourself with the truth. Jesus said, *"Thy [God's] word is truth"* (John 17:17). Satan is the liar and father of lies. Determine in your heart that having done all to stand, you will stand fire on God's Word. You will not be moved by what you see, hear or think. You are only moved by the Word of God.

Of the man who delights in God's Word, making it final authority, Psalm 112:6-8 says: *"Surely he shall not be moved for ever: the righteous shall be in everlasting remembrance. He shall not be afraid of evil tidings: his heart is fixed, trusting in the Lord. His heart is established, he shall not be afraid, until he see his desire upon his enemies."*

Fix your attention on God's Word. Trust only in the Lord and not in the evil reports you hear. Establish your heart in the Word of God!

The breastplate of righteousness has a particular meaning to you as a believer. It was no accident that the Spirit of God chose the breastplate to represent righteousness. Without the breastplate, vital areas of a soldier's are exposed to his enemy. Without righteousness, the vital parts of your prayer life are exposed to Satan.

Righteousness may well be the most misunderstood subject in the New Testament. To the religious mind, righteousness is good, moral conduct. The true meaning, however, is very different. *Righteousness* is simply right-standing with God. Because of that right-standing, you have rights and privileges in His kingdom.

You will become more aware of those rights and privileges as you realize what happens when you make Jesus the Lord of your life. There are two spiritual families: the family of God and the family of the devil.

For I reckon that the sufferings of this present time are not worthy to be compared with the glory which shall be revealed in us (Romans 8:18).

Ye are of your father the devil, and the lusts of your father ye will do. He was a murderer from the beginning, and abode not in the truth, because there is no truth in him. When he speaketh a lie, he speaketh of his own: for he is a liar, and the father if it (John 8:44).

Wherein in time past ye walked according to the course of this world, according to the prince of the power of the air, the spirit that now worketh in the children of disobedience: Among whom also we had our conversation in times past in the lusts of our flesh, fulfilling the desires of the flesh and of the mind; and were by nature the children of wrath, even as other (Ephesians 2:2-3).

Your faith in Jesus gives you power to become a child of God. When you make Jesus the Lord of your life, your spirit is born again. You no longer belong to Satan's kingdom. You are translated into the kingdom of God's Son (Colossians 1:12-13). **You are now an heir of God and a joint heir with Jesus Christ! What is His is yours. You have His righteousness! This is your breastplate!** It makes you worthy in the sight of God.

As long as you see yourself unworthy, you will not experience answered prayer to any heart degree. An understanding of righteousness will put you on the road to success. You have aright to resist Satan and to expect him to flee.

Believers all over the world are learning their rights. They are becoming more and more aware of their position as children of God and joint heirs with Jesus (Romans 8:17). They are taking advantage of the breastplate of righteousness!

Your next piece of armor is for your feet. They are to be shod with the preparation of the gospel of peace. Jesus said, *"Go ye into all the world, and preach the gospel to every creature"* (Mark 16:15). The gospel is the good news that we have peace through Jesus Christ. Isaiah 52:7 says, *"How beautiful upon the mountains are the feet of him that bringeth good tidings, that publisheth peace."* Sharing the gospel with others is part of your armor.

The Word says, *"Above all, taking the shield of faith."* Your shield quenches all of the fiery darts of the wicked! First John 5:4 says, *"…And this is the victory that over cometh the world, even our faith."* Your faith makes you an overcomer and more than a conqueror! *"The just shall live by faith"* (Romans 1:17). This mean your whole life is sustained by your faith in God.

Finally, *"Take the helmet of salvation."* A helmet is protection for the head. Romans 12:2 says, *"And be not conformed to this world: but be ye transformed by the renewing of your mind, that ye may prove what is that good, and acceptable, and perfect, will of God."* Satan's battleground is your mind. By keeping your mind renewed to the Word of God, you will protect it from Satan's onslaught of doubt and unbelief. This is closely related to having your loins girt with the truth. Freedom is the truth. Jesus said, *"If ye continue in my word, then are ye my disciples indeed; And ye shall know the truth, and the truth shall make you free"* (John 8:31-32). The key is *continuing*. You cannot just try this. You must make a quality decision to do it. You will then experience the freedom from Satan that is rightfully yours as a child of God.

Your armor is the same spiritual armor that Jesus wore during His earthly ministry. *"And he saw that there was no man, and wondered that there was no intercessor: Therefore his arm brought salvation unto him; and his righteousness, it sustained him. For he put on righteousness as a breastplate, and an helmet of salvation upon his head; and he put on the garments of vengeance for clothing, and was clad with zeal as a cloak"* (Isaiah 59:16-17). He proved it before He gave it to you. It worked proficiently for Him. Why? Because He was here for one purpose – to fulfill God's will in the earth. Jesus ministered on earth as a prophet under the Abrahamic covenant. Philippians 2:8 says that Jesus humbled Himself. In the original Greek, that literally says, *"He emptied Himself of His divine privileges.* He walked as a man, filled with the Holy Ghost. Jesus said, *"I can of mine own self do nothing: as I hear, I judge: and my judgment is just; because I seek not mine own will, but the will of the Father which hath sent me"* (John 5:30). He wore this armor as a man and then He gave it to the Church!

God has set in motion a security system on earth. This system is prayer. It includes the whole armor of God and the weapons of our warfare. The principles involved are designed to put a padlock on Satan's forces. This gives the Spirit of God an avenue through which He can carry out God's will in the lives of His people.

The armor we have talked about has been defensive. Let's look at our offensive weapons! Ephesians 6:17 says that the Word of God is the sword of the Spirit. To handle your sword skillfully, you need to know how the Word works. It will bring results. Satan will retreat from its blows in terror!

In mark 4, Jesus likens the Word to God to seed sown in the ground. When you plant seed, it produces a corp. You do not plant corn, expecting to grow apples or bananas. When corn is planted, corn will grow, so it is with the Word of God. When you plant the Word in your heart, it will grow produce.

Your life – like soil – will produce what is sown in it. Plant seeds of doubt, fear, unbelief and failure and you can expect to produce a crop of doubt, fear, unbelief and failure in your life. You cannot plant seeds of doubt expecting to produce faith. It simply will not work.

The Word is sharper than a two-edged sword piercing and dividing asunder the soul and the spirit, the joints and the marrow (Hebrews 4:12). The Word goes beyond your intellect. It enters the spirit realm. Only doubt and unbelief will stop the Word from operating in your behalf. When you plant the Word concerning healing in your heart, then you will produce a harvest to healing IF doubt and fear do not enter and ruin your corp.

Jesus said, *"The sower soweth the word…but when they have heard, Satan cometh immediately, and taketh away the word that was sown in their hearts"* (Mark 4:14-15). Satan comes immediately to steal the Word. You have to guard against his maneuvers. The best way to combat an enemy is to familiarize yourself with his tactics. Once you know how Satan operates, you will be able to defeat him.

When a man plants seed in the ground, he does not go out a few days later and dig it up to see if it is growing. Seeds never produce that way. He has to have faith in the seed's ability to grow and produce.

Faith in the Word works the same way. When you are believing God for healing, and symptoms linger, you do not give up and say, "Well, I guess it didn't work for me." That's what Satan would like you to do. You have to continually water the ground and cultivate it with the Word until the seed is able to sprout and grow. Don't dig up your seed!

If a farmer placed his seed on a shelf, it would never produce. He must put the seed in its correct environment for the life in it to come forth. The Word must be treated as that seed. If you need healing, then plant the seed of God's Word concerning healing in the correct environment –your heart. When your Bible is left lying on a bookshelf, it will be of no use to you.

Not spending time in the Word when you are fighting a spiritual battle would be like leaving your sword in its sheath while you are on the battlefield. Take your Bible down from the shelf and feed the Word into your heart. Spend time meditating in the Word until the seed of healing can grow and develop and bring forth the desired fruit in your life.

When a seed is planted in the ground and cultivated, it will take root. The shoot will force its way to the surface. When the plant blooms, it will produce many more just like it. **The Word, like a seed has the power within itself to grow and bear fruit.**

Propect the Word until it has time to take root and grow. Rule over your thought life by casting down imaginations that exalt themselves against the Word. To be carnally minded or sense-ruled is death (Romans 8:6). It will kill you. To spiritually minded is *life* and peace. Keep your thoughts on the Word. It is the answer to your problem. You will experience life and peace by keep the end result on your mind and thus protecting the seed of God's Word. The Word of God works only when it is put to work. Submit yourselves to God (James 4:7). Resist the devil and he WILL flee from you!

God has provided a strong arsenal for spiritual warfare. The Word is not your only weapon against Satan.

When you pray in Jesus' Name, you immediately get the ear of God. At the same time, you get Satan's attention.

The Name of Jesus carries ultimate authority in the spirit world. Philippians 2:9-10 says, "...*God also hath highly exalted him, and given* *a name which is above every name: That at the name of Jesus every knee should bow, of things in heaven, and things in earth, and things under the earth."* In Jesus' Name, the believer has authority to *"…tread on serpents and scorpions and over all the power of the enemy"* (Luke 10:19). Satan knows the power vested in that Name and he will retreat when it is spoken in faith (James 4:7). One translation says to stand up to the devil and he will turn and run!

Let's look at Hebrews 1:3-4: *"Who being the brightness of his glory, and the express image of his person, and upholding all things by the word of his power, when he had himself purged our sins, sat down on the right hand of the Majesty on high; Being made so much better than the angels, as he hath by inheritance obtained a more excellent name than they."* If the Name of Jesus is more excellent than that of the angels in good standing with God, how much more would it be than the name of Satan? He is a fallen angel!

Before He ascended into heaven, Jesus commissioned His disciples to go into all the earth. He said, "All power has been given unto me both in heaven and in earth. Therefore, YOU go into all the earth. IN MY NAME lay hands on the sick and they will recover. IN MY NAME cast out the devil. Just as a wife has power of attorney to her husband's name, we have been given Jesus' Name to use in combat against Satan. We have authority to speak His Name in His stead.

When Peter and John ministered to the man at the gate Beautiful, they spoke in the Name of Jesus. Peter said, *"Silver and gold have I none; but such as I have give I thee: In the name of Jesus Christ of Nazareth rise up and walk"* (Acts 3:6). Later he explained what had happened. Peter said,

…Ye men of Israel, why marvel ye at this?

Or why look ye so earnestly on us, as though by our own power or holiness we had made this man to walk? The God of Abraham, and

of Isaac, and of Jacob, the God of our fathers, hath glorified his Son Jesus...And his name through faith in his name hath made this man strong, whom ye see and know: yea, the faith which is by him hath given him this perfect soundness in the presence of you all (Acts 3:12-13, 16).

Peter was simply using the authority Jesus had given him only a few days before. The early apostles did not have special power in themselves to do mighty works. Their holiness didn't make them special. They didn't even have the written New Testament. All they could do was speak Jesus' Name in faith and the Holy Spirit did the mighty works. The fabulous earthshaking revival of the early Church was sparked by only one commandment: "Go in the Name of Jesus." The power vested in Jesus' Name has *never* changed.

Most believers know that it is the Name of Jesus that caused them to be saved. The Bible says, *"...Whosoever shall call upon the Name of the Lord shall be saved."* He is rich unto those that call upon his name (Romans 10:12-13). When you call upon some one's name, you are placing a demand on their ability. For instance, when a policeman says, "Halt in the name of the law!" he is being backed by the power of that particular city. It is as if the entire corporate structure of that city is speaking. He is carrying out the power behind the name of the law.

To know how much confidence you can place in a name, you must be able to measure the power behind it. A man writing a check places a demand on his name. If he has the proper funds in the bank, then there is enough power to meet the demand.

The power backing the Name of Jesus is the power of Almighty God! First John 3:22-23 says, *"And whatsoever we ask, we receive of him, because we keep his commandments, and do those things that are pleasing in his sight. And this is his commandment, that we should believe on the name of his Son Jesus Christ, and love one another, as he gave us commandment."* We have a commandment to believer on the Name of the Son of God.

To believer on His name is to put demand upon His ability. Jesus said, *"Whatsoever ye shall ask the Father in my name, he will give it you"* (John 16:23). The mighty, powerful Name of Jesus is available to you. Become aware of your right and privilege to use it. Ask the Holy Spirit to engrave the reality of it in your heart. His ministry is to lead you into all truth (John 16:13).

The Names of Jesus is the Key to heaven's storehouse. It can do anything that Jesus can do. Speaking His Name is standing in His stead. According to Philippians 2:9-11, the entire spectrum of existence – heaven, earth, under the earth – will bow its knee and confess with its mouth that Jesus is Lord to the glory of God the Father. The Name of Jesus is a name that is above every name. Upon being raised from the dead, Jesus inherited the very name of God (Hebrews 1:4). To measure the power behind His Name, you would have to measure that power of almighty God. It cannot be done. His power is measureless and He wants to use it in our behalf.

God's love motivates Him to use His power. First John 4:16 says, *"And we have know and believed the love that God hath to us…"* When you *believe* the love that God has for you, then you will begin to realize that you have as much right to use the Name of Jesus as anyone else. Believe the love that God has for you.

Once you recognize the reality of God's love in your life, you will realize that He has not left you defenseless and powerless against evil. God covered the entire spectrum of Satan's existence with the power invested in the mighty Name of Jesus.!

Another essential of our spiritual warfare is the Holy Spirit. Before He went to the cross, Jesus promised to send Him. We have armor and weapons, but it is the Holy Spirit Who empowers us to utilize them.

The Holy Spirit is the power of God. The effectiveness of your prayer life depends on the degree of confidence you place in the Holy Spirit.

He is the power behind your prayers that enables you to live and walk as God intends – free from sin, sickness, sorrow and death. He dwells within you. You may not be aware of His presence, but He is there. The Holy Spirit fills a vital role in your prayer life. Pray to the Father in Jesus' Name, not to the Holy Spirit. He is in you – creating, energizing, working – to perform the will of God in your life. By operating on the Word of God, you will see the work of the Holy Spirit. He will do exceeding abundantly beyond what we can even as or think according to the power that is at work within us (Ephesians 3:20). The Holy Spirit is that power.

He is your helper, sent to bear you up. He has come to your aid to give you might in your inner man. He is in you, instantly ready to do the bidding of God and to uphold the Name of Jesus.

The operation of the Holy Spirit should be a reality to you. When you invite Him into your life, you receive more than just an experience. The Holy Spirit of God came to abide with you forever. He is residing inside you constantly. He is real and He wants to help you in your prayer life.

www.ingramcontent.com/pod-product-compliance
Ingram Content Group UK Ltd.
Pitfield, Milton Keynes, MK11 3LW, UK
UKHW022227230426